# Anointed in the Spirit

## Candidate Handbook

# Anointed in the Spirit

## Candidate Handbook

A Middle School Confirmation Program

Rita Burns Senseman

saint mary's press

The Subcommittee on the Catechism, United States Conference of Catholic Bishops, has found this catechetical text, copyright 2010, to be in conformity with the *Catechism of the Catholic Church.*

Nihil Obstat:     Rev. William M. Becker, STD
                  Censor Librorum
                  November 13, 2009
Imprimatur:       Most Rev. John M. Quinn, DD
                  Bishop of Winona
                  November 13, 2009

The nihil obstat and imprimatur are official declarations that a book or pamphlet is free of doctrinal or moral error. No implication is contained therein that those who have granted the nihil obstat or imprimatur agree with the contents, opinions, or statements expressed, nor do they assume any legal responsibility associated with publication.

The publishing team included Maura Thompson Hagarty, development editor; prepress and manufacturing coordinated by the production departments of Saint Mary's Press.

Printed in the United States of America

2820  (PO5465)


ISBN 978-0-88489-814-6, Print

# Contents

# You're Invited!

This is an invitation to celebrate the Sacrament of Confirmation. This isn't an ordinary invitation to just any celebration. You are invited to complete your Christian initiation by receiving a special outpouring of the Holy Spirit.

God created you in his image through love, and he continues to love you. God is always calling you to communion with him and wants you to find happiness. Celebrating Confirmation strengthens your relationship with God—the Father, the Son, and the Holy Spirit—and helps you to live a life of faith!

# Welcome!

## About This Handbook

This book has been created to make your preparation for Confirmation enjoyable, fruitful, and memorable. Here is what you will find in this book:

## A Walk Through the Order of Confirmation

The chapters of this book introduce you to central aspects of the Confirmation liturgy and help you to explore the meaning of the Sacrament. The material will help you to deepen your understanding of God's call to you to live a life of faith and to explore the significance of being confirmed Catholic.

## Special Features

Each chapter includes a number of special features designed to enhance your preparation. These include the following sidebars:

### Jesus Connection

These sidebars help you learn more about who Jesus is and how he is central to our faith and to the Sacrament of Confirmation.

### Dear God

The "Dear God" feature offers a short prayer for you to pray on your own and with others during your preparation sessions.

### Did You Know?

These sidebars explore topics related to Confirmation that complement the main chapter material.

### Catholic Connection

The "Catholic Connection" sidebars help you to review some of the central teachings of the Church.

### Right from the Rite

This feature presents quotations from the *Order of Confirmation* and other rites of the Church. A rite is an official liturgical celebration, such as the Rite of Baptism for Children and the Order of Confirmation.

### Words from the Word

The "Words from the Word" are Scripture quotations.

### My Mission

The "My Mission" feature invites you to record ideas for how to live as a follower of Jesus who is filled with the Holy Spirit.

### Journaling

Each chapter ends with a journal page that includes suggestions for reflection. If your leader or catechist doesn't invite you to complete these pages during your sessions, you can complete them on your own.

You are part of the Communion of Saints. Call to mind a few of the saints who are most meaningful to you.

## Catholic Prayers and Beliefs

At the end of this handbook, you will find a handy collection of prayers and summaries of Catholic beliefs and practices in two separate appendixes.

## Saints

Another feature you will find at the end of the book is a list of saints. The list is organized according to causes and groups. These are the special causes or groups of people the saints have been linked to in the Church's tradition. Also included are the saints' feast days. This list may be helpful if you consider choosing a new name for Confirmation (see the section titled "Your Confirmation Name").

# Overview of the Preparation Program

Every parish does Confirmation preparation a little bit differently, but here are several activities you may be invited to participate in beyond preparation sessions with your fellow candidates:

- orientation sessions for parents, sponsors, and candidates
- conversations with your sponsor
- a retreat
- a celebration of the Sacrament of Penance and Reconciliation
- activities that promote justice or provide a service to people in need
- a rehearsal for Confirmation

Your leader or catechist will provide you with detailed information about your parish's program. He or she will also talk to you about choosing a sponsor and a Confirmation name.

# Your Confirmation Sponsor

Choosing a Confirmation sponsor is an important decision for candidates. Spend some time thinking about whom you will choose, praying about your choice, and talking with a parent.

If feasible, your sponsor for Confirmation should be one of your godparents from Baptism. This helps to show the close relationship between your Baptism and your Confirmation. Plus, it makes sense because your godparents have made a commitment to help and support you in your Christian life. And that's exactly what a Confirmation sponsor does! A Confirmation sponsor helps and supports you in being a faithful disciple of Jesus Christ.

You do, however, have the option of choosing someone other than a godparent. The Church says a Confirmation sponsor is a person who . . .

- is at least sixteen years of age (unless your diocese has established a different age)
- has been confirmed and has received the Eucharist
- is a practicing Catholic in good standing with the Church

Here are a few questions that may help you choose your Confirmation sponsor:

- If both godparents are available to sponsor you, is one of them a better choice for a Confirmation sponsor?
- Is the person a good role model for the Catholic way of life?
- Does the person have time to spend with you as you prepare for Confirmation? Is he or she available to come to the rehearsal and the celebration of Confirmation? (Even if the person can't come, he or she might

still be a good sponsor. Check with your leader or catechist about this.)

- Would you feel comfortable talking about your faith with this person?

If you have any questions, talk to your catechist or the leader of your preparation program.

Your Confirmation sponsor is a role model who guides you in the Catholic way of life. And, is someone you can talk to about your faith. Who do you think would be a good sponsor?

© Carmen Martinez/istockphoto.com

# Your Confirmation Name

When you are confirmed, the bishop will say, "*(your name)*, be sealed with the Gift of the Holy Spirit (*Order of Confirmation*, number 27)." There are two main practices regarding the name the bishop will say. The first is to use your baptismal name. The second is to select a new name. Your catechist or program leader will give you guidance about your options.

## Baptismal Name

During your preparation for Confirmation, you will hear a lot about the close relationship between Baptism and Confirmation. You will learn that Confirmation completes the process of initiation that was begun in Baptism. You will also learn that the outpouring of the Holy Spirit in Confirmation perfects the grace you received in Baptism. When Confirmation candidates are confirmed using their baptismal names, the close connection between Baptism and Confirmation is highlighted.

## New Name

In some parishes and dioceses, candidates have the option of selecting new names for Confirmation or using their baptismal names. If you consider selecting a new name, a good approach is to choose the name of a saint or a holy person whose life inspires you to live faithfully. This name can be a symbol of what you will strive for in your life as a confirmed Catholic.

# 1 Being a Candidate

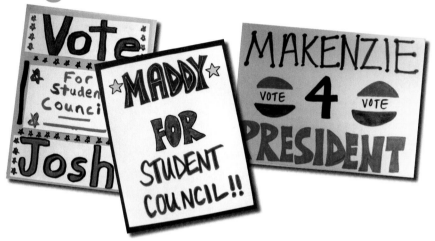

Have you ever run for student council at your school? or maybe you know someone who was a candidate for student council? Have you or your parents ever publicly supported a candidate for mayor or maybe even for president? Being a candidate is a big deal!

Why is being a candidate such a big deal? A candidate is someone who is being considered for something important like a leadership position or an award. Perhaps you've had a coach who was a candidate for a coach-of-the-year award or a friend who was a candidate for a science award. If you are a candidate for something, then chances are it's a pretty big deal. And that's the case here. You are a candidate for the Sacrament of Confirmation. That is definitely a big deal!

Like most important things, being a candidate involves some work and comes with some responsibilities. For example, if you were a candidate for president of the United States, you would have to campaign and let people know why you would be a good president. If you were a candidate for student council, you would tell your classmates why you should be elected. You might say: "I am a hard worker and very trustworthy. I promise to bring your ideas to the council."

Being a candidate for the Sacrament of Confirmation is different though, because you don't campaign. You don't have to be voted in or elected. God has already elected or chosen you

through Baptism. Any baptized person who reaches the appropriate age can and should become a candidate for Confirmation. Everyone is encouraged to be confirmed, because without Confirmation a person's Christian initiation is incomplete. Confirmation adds to the gift of new life we receive in Baptism. Confirmation is like getting an extra gift. It deepens the gift of the Holy Spirit we receive in Baptism.

## Your Confirmation Candidacy

When you are a candidate for Confirmation, you are in a period of preparation for receiving the Sacrament. You have a special place in the Church, and your parish community has a responsibility to help you get ready for Confirmation.

# My Mission

## A Candidate's Mission

Now that you are a candidate for Confirmation, your mission is to prepare yourself for the celebration of the Sacrament. What will you do to prepare?

## What the Parish Promises

Here are some of the things the parish promises to help you with while you are preparing for Confirmation:

- developing a closer relationship with God—the Father, the Son, and the Holy Spirit
- becoming more familiar with the presence and action of the Holy Spirit in your life
- gaining a stronger sense of belonging to the Church—your parish as well as the worldwide or universal Church
- developing greater capability to serve others and contribute to the Church's mission

Be assured that members of your parish will also be praying for you.

© Bill Wittman

The Church stands with you as you prepare for Confirmation. Members of your parish will help you along the way. What might fellow parishioners do for you?

# What *Is* Asked of You

Even though candidates for Confirmation do not campaign, the Church does ask that you be prepared and that you meet certain requirements. Here's a checklist of guidelines:

## A Candidate's Checklist

- ❏ I am baptized.
- ❏ I have not been confirmed before.
- ❏ I am over the age of seven (or other age set by my bishop).
- ❏ I want to live as a disciple of Christ and be a witness to the Christian way of life for others.
- ❏ I am willing to seek guidance about the Christian life from my Confirmation sponsor.
- ❏ I want to receive the Sacrament of Confirmation and complete my initiation into the Church, which began with my Baptism.
- ❏ I am willing to pray more often in order to be better prepared to receive the Gifts of the Holy Spirit in Confirmation.

- ❏ I am capable of renewing my baptismal promises. (We'll talk more about baptismal promises in chapter 3.)
- ❏ I am willing to receive the Sacrament of Penance and Reconciliation before receiving Confirmation to make sure I am in the state of grace (see the "Did You Know?" feature on page 24).
- ❏ I attend Mass.
- ❏ I am willing to spend time preparing for the Sacrament of Confirmation and learning more about its meaning and significance for my life.

Your parish or diocese probably has some additional guidelines or requirements, so check with your catechist or parish leader.

## Right from the Rite

"Those who have been baptized continue on the path of Christian initiation through the Sacrament of Confirmation, by which they receive the outpouring of the Holy Spirit, whom the Lord sent upon the Apostles at Pentecost." (*Order of Confirmation*, number 1)

## What God Promises

First and foremost, God promises love. Because he loves us, God has revealed to us that he is one God in three Persons: the Trinity. This is the central mystery of Christianity. The three divine Persons—the Father, the Son, and the Holy Spirit—are completely in union with one another, and their love flows out to us. God has given himself to us and calls us to share in the love and life of the Trinity.

God desires that we will respond to his Revelation with faith. Faith is first of all a gift from God. Someone cannot have faith without the Holy Spirit, who helps us see our need for God. Being free to choose our response to this gift is part of our nature as humans. Being faithful is possible when someone understands and freely chooses to believe in God and his Church. Our salvation depends on our faith.

Having faith means that we believe. Believing is also an act of the entire Church. Don't confuse Church—with a capital C—with a building. The Church is the community of faithful people who put their faith in Jesus Christ. It is the Church that teaches you. It is the Church that is a role model for you. It is the Church that supports and nourishes your own faith.

One part of a faith-filled response to God is to complete your initiation into the Church by being confirmed. Through the waters of Baptism and the action of the Holy Spirit, we become members of Christ's Body, the Church. God continues to call us throughout our lives to deepen our relationship with him and strengthen our bond with the Church.

In the Sacrament of Confirmation, there is a special outpouring of the Holy Spirit upon those being confirmed. Through the action of the Holy Spirit, the Father, united with Christ, accomplishes great things for us:

- Our relationship with the Father grows deeper.
- We are united more firmly to Jesus Christ.
- The Gifts of the Holy Spirit increase in us.
- Our connection with the Church increases, and we are better able to continue the Church's mission.
- The Holy Spirit gives us a special strength to be witnesses to the Christian way of life through what we say and what we do.

And, rest assured, God always keeps his promises! So even if you don't do all the things you say you'll do, God will always do what he says. God's promises are trustworthy and eternal.

We do not have to earn God's gifts. That is not at all the point of spending some time in preparation as a candidate for Confirmation. The time of preparation is meant to help candidates be receptive to the outpouring of the Holy Spirit. God calls each of us at all times and pours out his love upon us. The challenge for us is to recognize his love and his call and to respond with faithful living.

# Called by God

The Scriptures are filled with accounts of people who heard God's call and responded with faith. Here are a few of those people and the verses where you can read about them.

| Biblical People | Scripture Verses |
|---|---|
| Abraham | Genesis 12:1–9 |
| Moses | Exodus 3:1–12 |
| Samuel | 1 Samuel 3:1–10 |
| Isaiah | Isaiah 6:1–8 |
| Jeremiah | Jeremiah 1:4–10 |
| Mary | Luke 1:26—38 |
| The First Disciples | Matthew 4:18–22 |
| Matthew | Matthew 9:9–13 |
| The Samaritan Woman | John 4:4–42 |
| Saul | Acts of the Apostles 9:1–19 |

© Brooklyn Museum/Corbis

Jesus approached the tax collector Matthew, considered a sinner by many, at his collection booth. "Follow me," Jesus called. How will you answer Jesus' call?

## Candidates for Sacraments

You and your peers who are Confirmation candidates are most likely not the only candidates in your parish responding to God's call by preparing for initiation Sacraments. Parents of babies are preparing to present them for Baptism. Children are getting ready for First Communion. Adults who didn't complete their initiation when they were young might now be seeking Confirmation. Catechumens, both adults and children older than seven, are seeking to join the Church and are candidates for all three Sacraments of Christian Initiation: Baptism, Confirmation, and the Eucharist.

There is also another type of candidate for the Sacraments of Christian Initiation. These people are candidates for reception into the full communion of the Catholic Church. These candidates are already baptized, but not as Catholics. They are Christian and might be Methodist, Baptist, Lutheran, or Episcopalian, for example. When these kinds of baptized candidates join the Catholic Church, they usually receive Confirmation and the Eucharist during the same liturgy.

Whether a person is young or old, baptized or unbaptized, Catholic already or just becoming Catholic, Confirmation is an essential part of becoming a full member of the Catholic Church.

Let's turn now from the different types of candidates and take a look at your Confirmation candidacy.

# Catholic Connection

## The Seven Sacraments

Confirmation is one of the Church's Seven Sacraments. The other six are Baptism, the Eucharist, Penance and Reconciliation, Anointing of the Sick, Holy Orders, and Matrimony.

The Sacraments bring us face to face with God. We don't literally "see" God in a visual way, but we know he is with us and loves us. We call this relationship with God grace. We encounter grace most fully in the Sacraments. Through grace we participate in God's divine life, the life of the Trinity. It is pure love between the Father and the Son poured out to us by the Holy Spirit. When we celebrate Sacraments with the required disposition, an attitude of openness to God's love, we are able to recognize his presence more clearly. The Sacraments truly make present the graces that they signify. For example, in Baptism, the person really becomes a new creation.

The Sacraments are gifts from Christ, who instituted them. The Gospels show us how he established the meaning of each Sacrament and commissioned his disciples the celebrate them.

The Sacraments fall into three categories:

1. **Baptism, Confirmation, and the Eucharist** are the Sacraments of Christian Initiation because they are the foundation of Christian life. Baptism is the first Sacrament celebrated because it makes us members of Christ and part of the Church. Confirmation strengthens us and is necessary to complete baptismal grace. The Eucharist nourishes us with Christ's Body and Blood and completes Christian initiation. It is the high point of Christian life and all the Sacraments are oriented toward it.

2. **Anointing of the Sick and Penance and Reconciliation** are the Sacraments of Healing because through them the Church continues Jesus' mission to heal and forgive sins.

3. **Holy Orders and Matrimony** are the Sacraments at the Service of Communion. These Sacraments contribute to the Church's mission primarily through service to others.

## Jesus Connection

### Jesus of Nazareth

It was Jesus of Nazareth who called Zacchaeus down from the tree. Jesus wasn't just a regular guy passing through Jericho, but he may have looked like one. He had a human nature, like ours. He experienced pain and joy. He laughed and cried. He went through childhood and all the periods of human development, like us. We can imagine him as a child hanging out with friends and learning carpentry from Joseph.

Jesus is fully man, like all of us, except he did not sin. But that's not all. There is much more to understanding Jesus' identity. He is a divine Person, the second Person of the Trinity, who took on a human nature. That doesn't mean he is half man and half God. "He became truly man while remaining truly God. Jesus Christ is true God and true man" (*Catechism of the Catholic Church* [*CCC*], number 464).

## Confirmation During the Teen Years

Most Confirmation candidates in the United States celebrated Baptism as babies and the Eucharist at around age seven or grade two, and then celebrate Confirmation during the middle school or high school years. The celebration follows the Order of Confirmation. That's what the Church calls the official Confirmation ceremony. The Anointed in the Spirit program will help you prepare by walking you through various parts of the Order of Confirmation and helping you explore its rich meaning and significance. Our walk-through begins in this chapter with the Presentation of the Candidates.

## Presentation of the Candidates

Confirmation is normally celebrated within the Mass. This helps to show the connection between Confirmation and the other two Sacraments of Christian Initiation, Baptism and the Eucharist. Whether celebrated within or outside of the Mass, however, there is a celebration of the Word, called the Liturgy of the Word, before the Order of Confirmation. Hearing the Word is very important because the Holy Spirit flows out among all the people gathered and makes God's will known in their lives.

After the proclamation of the Gospel, the Order of Confirmationitself begins with the Presentation of the Candidates. The bishop sits down instead of going right into his homily. The candidates are then presented to the bishop by a leader in the community, such as a priest, deacon, or catechist.

## Called by Name

Each candidate is called by name, if possible. As the priest, deacon, or catechist calls out a person's name, she or he stands. If the group is large, calling each individual name may not be feasible. If each person is not called by name, all the candidates stand before the bishop as a group. However, there is great meaning in being called by name. Let's take a closer look.

How many times a day do you hear your name called? Cameron! Samantha! Austin! Kylie! Who calls you by name? Your mom? your dad? your friends? your teacher? your bus driver? your coach? Hearing your name called means something's up. Your friend wants you to come over. Your dad wants to know if your homework is done. Your mom wants you to hurry up and get in the car! Your coach wants you to get to the ball faster. Your grandmother wants you to know she loves you.

When the Church calls you by name, it means God wants you. God is calling you. Being called by name is personal. You are called out, singled out of the crowd. You are not just part of the pack anymore. God invites you personally into relationship.

Remember how Jesus called Zacchaeus the tax collector by name (see Luke 19:1–10). Zacchaeus was part of a big crowd, watching Jesus from a distance. He climbed a tree so he could

"When he reached the place, Jesus looked up and said to him, 'Zacchaeus, come down quickly, for today I must stay at your house.'" (Luke 19:5)

© Brooklyn Museum, Purchased by public subscription

Jesus singled out Zacchaeus in a very personal way, calling him by name. Through the Church, God calls you by name in Confirmation.

# Did You Know?

## The State of Grace

Grace is the gift of God's loving presence in our lives. It is the help he gives us through the Holy Spirit to participate in God's life. God wants us to be with him. At Baptism we receive the life of the Holy Spirit. The Spirit breathes love into us. This gift of grace draws us into close relationship with God the Father and Jesus Christ and gives us the help we need to become God's adopted sons and daughters.

The Church says that you must be in the "state of grace" to receive the Sacrament of Confirmation. Nothing we can do will ever stop God from loving us. When we talk about being in the state of grace, we mean being open to God's gift and responding to God's call. It doesn't mean perfect living, free from all sin every day. But to be in the state of grace is to be free from serious sin, the kind that turns us away from God and shows that we have rejected his love. These kinds of sins are called mortal sins because they bring spiritual death. Less serious sins are called venial sins.

Before receiving Confirmation, the Church asks that you receive the Sacrament of Penance and Reconciliation. Through this Sacrament, God forgives your sins. Even if you haven't committed any serious sins' the Sacrament is important for your life. The grace of the Sacrament strengthens our relationship with God and the Church and helps us resist our tendency to sin. The Sacrament helps to prepare Confirmation candidates to receive, with open hearts and minds, the Gifts of the Holy Spirit.

When you receive the Sacrament of Confirmation, God's own self will be poured out through the Holy Spirit. You will be filled with the gift of God's loving presence even more than you already are!

see Jesus, and when Jesus approached, he called out to Zacchaeus by name. It was up to Zacchaeus to respond, and he did. His encounter with Jesus changed his life.

When God calls each of us, it is personal. He wants us to respond, and he gives us the grace that enables us to do so.

### Standing Before the Bishop

So there you'll be, called by name and standing before the bishop. The bishop is the minister of Confirmation. (We'll talk more about him in chapter 6.)

After you've been called, the bishop will give the homily. He'll explain the Scripture readings and talk about the meaning of Confirmation.

After the homily, the bishop will ask you some questions. But that's for the next chapter. For now let's concentrate on what it means to be a candidate.

## Being a Candidate

A candidate is a person preparing for something important. You've been called by God to prepare for Confirmation. It's a big deal. Take it seriously. But also enjoy all the special support from your parish, your sponsor, and your family as you prepare to be confirmed. You won't be a candidate for too long. Confirmation will be here before you know it!

**Dear God**

You call all people of
the earth to yourself.
You have called me to be a
candidate for Confirmation.
Help me to answer your
call by being the best
candidate I can possibly be.
I pray that during this time
I'll come closer to you and
your Son, Jesus Christ.
I pray that the Holy Spirit
will help me and guide
me in all I do.
Amen.

# Responding to the Call

You hear your name called several times a day. But God's call is a bit different. God is calling you to the Sacrament of Confirmation and to a life of Christian discipleship. Read about some of the people from the Bible listed in the "Called by God" sidebar on page 19. Record insights from the Scripture passages that may help you to be a faithful disciple.

# 2 Baptism: Waters of New Life

What comes to your mind when you think about water—swimming, waterslides, a warm bath or shower, walking along the seashore, rainy days, mud puddles, water bottles, water balloons, drinking fountains, fishing, boating? Maybe some less positive things come to mind too, like flooding, hurricanes, stories of people getting caught in strong currents?

© Steve Cole/Anyone/amanaimages/Corbis

Cool rainwater on your skin makes you feel alive and free. In what way is the water of Baptism associated with life and freedom?

## Water Brings Life and Death

Water is a source of life. We drink it every day. It's in our sports drinks and orange juice. It's in most everything we drink and eat, and we need it to survive. We cook with it, bathe with it, and play in it. You've probably heard that approximately two-thirds of the human body is made up of water and that approximately 70 percent of the earth's surface is covered with water. Water is absolutely essential for life.

At the same time, water can bring destruction, and even death. Thousands of people die each year in drowning accidents. Hurricane Katrina destroyed lives and homes in New Orleans and along the Gulf Coast. Floods, tsunamis, and cyclones kill people and wipe out property all over the world. Severe storms and floods may have done damage not too far from where you live. You may even be a bit frightened when a severe thunderstorm hits your area.

Water can be scary, but it can also be beautiful and enjoyable. A white sandy beach with the sun setting over the water is a magnificent sight. But that same water could take your life.

Water brings us joy, refreshment, and life, but it also can bring death and destruction. The waters of Baptism do the same. They bring both life and death. In Baptism the water is a sacramental symbol that signifies what God does in the Sacrament. By the power of the Holy Spirit, God gives us new life in Christ and makes us a new creation. We are born anew and made members of Christ's Body, the Church.

Baptismal waters are also associated with destruction. Through Baptism the Holy Spirit destroys sin and death. By the power of the Holy Spirit, the waters of Baptism wash away all sins, both Original Sin and personal sin, as well as the punishment for sin.

© Tony Campbell /istockphoto.com

Water is very powerful and can be destructive. How could new life come forth from the devastation caused by this flood? In Baptism, how does new life come from death?

# Taking a Closer Look at Baptism

In all likelihood, you were baptized as a baby, because in the Catholic Church most people are baptized as infants. Since the early Church, Baptism has been celebrated with young children. We don't wait to baptize at an older age because we don't need to do anything to earn it. God's love is a pure gift to us. Nothing we could do at any age would make us more deserving of this gift than we already are at birth. The Church baptizes children in the faith of the Church with the hope that, as members of God's family, they will learn to love and respond to God.

If you were a baby or young child when you were baptized, ask your family to tell you about your Baptism. Reflecting on your Baptism and its meaning is a helpful step in preparing for Confirmation. Baptism comes first among all the Sacraments. It is the gateway to the Christian life. Let's try to imagine what your Baptism was like and explore its meaning.

## Right from the Rite

"My dear brothers and sisters, God uses the sacrament of water to give his divine life to those who believe in him. Let us turn to him, and ask him to pour his gift of life from this font on the children he has chosen." (*Order of Baptism for Children*, number 53)

## The Parish Welcomes the Children

First, try to imagine the place you were baptized. Most likely, you were baptized in a church, and it might have been the same church you attend today. Picture yourself arriving at the place of Baptism. Envision your parents, your godmother and godfather, and maybe even your grandparents, aunts, uncles, and cousins, all coming to church with you. Or, maybe it's just you and your mom and a godparent arriving for your Baptism. Imagine your family waiting for the priest to come and greet you.

One of the first things that would have happened at your Baptism is that the priest would have asked some questions. Guess what one of the first questions is? Here's a hint: In chapter 1, we talked about the importance of being called by name. Can you guess the question? It is "What name do you give your child?" Naming is so incredibly important. Your parents are presenting you to the community. The parish is receiving you by name. And God is claiming you to be his own—by name.

The priest also asks the parents what they are asking on behalf of their child. The parents reply, "Baptism," "faith," or something similar. Then the priest briefly reviews the parents' responsibilities for training their child in the practice of the faith and raising him or her to love God and neighbor. He then asks if they understand and asks the godparents if they are ready to help your parents. Next, the priest traces the cross on your forehead and then invites your parents and godparents to do the same. This signifies your new life in Christ and your new identity as a Christian.

# The Word of God at Baptism

After the welcoming and the signing with the cross comes the Liturgy of the Word. At Baptisms—and at all sacramental celebrations—the proclamation of God's Word and the homily are very important. Throughout our lives, the hearing of God's Word helps us to better recognize his love for us and keeps the faith of the Church alive.

Next come the Prayers of the Faithful. The community's prayers on the day of your Baptism included prayers for you, your family, and your friends. They may have called upon and remembered the saints. A prayer called the Litany of Saints is often prayed or sung during Baptism. The litany asks the saints to pray for us.

# Prayer of Exorcism and Anointing

After the Liturgy of the Word, there is a special prayer asking God to free you from sin. The prayer is called an exorcism.

### Prayer of Exorcism

An exorcism is a prayer for freedom from evil and the power of Satan, its instigator. The sin and evil in our world touch even a pure and innocent young child. So, the priest prays that a child being baptized will be freed from Original Sin (see the "Did You Know?" sidebar on page 32) and asks God to send the Holy Spirit to dwell with her or him.

### An Anointing

Did you know that Baptism can include two anointings with oil? The first is optional, so the priest can omit it if

# Did You Know?

## Original Sin

Every person but Jesus and Mary was conceived with Original Sin. This is a sinful condition that is part of fallen human nature. But how can a baby who never committed a sin have Original Sin? Where does it come from?

Adam and Eve, the first humans, were at peace with God and every other living thing, at first. Despite their happiness, they made the mistake of thinking they could be happy without God, and they disobeyed him. Because of their sinful choice, they lost their original holiness. This consequence affects the whole human race—except Jesus and Mary. This means we lack the freedom and holiness human beings were meant to have. Because of Original Sin, our human nature is weakened. We are influenced by ignorance, suffering, and knowledge of our own death. We're inclined to sin because our natural power for relating to God and choosing good is weakened.

Think about that for a second. Have you ever done something selfish or mean and later wondered why you did it? This gives you an idea about what an inclination to sin is. It is what makes us want to sometimes put our own pleasure ahead of doing.

You may think it is not fair for newborn children to have Original Sin, because they couldn't have done anything to deserve it. Original Sin is not a sin we commit. How it gets passed on from generation to generation is a mystery we do not fully understand.

Even though Original Sin affects us all, it does not mean we are born evil, and it does not stop us from returning to God. We have all been created in the image of God and have been offered his friendship. Through Baptism, the chief Sacrament for the forgiveness of sins, we are freed from Original Sin. We are washed clean and made new. God's power will always prevail over sin and evil. The washing away of Original Sin gave you a great start in life! You were united to Christ, who died and rose, freed from sin, and filled with the Holy Spirit.

he chooses. If he includes it, after the prayer of exorcism he asks Christ to strengthen the child and anoints him or her on the chest with blessed oil, called the oil of catechumens. You may recall from chapter 1 that a catechumen is a person who is preparing for the Sacrament of Baptism.

## The Celebration of Baptism

There is still more to do before a person is plunged into the waters or water is poured on her or him. If the water is not already blessed, the priest does so by asking the Father, through the Son, to send the power of the Holy Spirit upon the water so that the person being baptized will be "born of water and Spirit" (John 3:5). Then the priest asks the parents and godparents some questions about their faith. Because most candidates for Baptism are babies and thus too young to express faith, the priest wants to be sure that the main adults in the babies' lives have faith. This part is called the Profession of Faith or Renewal of Baptismal Promises. (At your Confirmation, you will be asked to renew your Baptismal Promises. We'll explore what that means in the next chapter.)

## The Water and the Holy Spirit

Once the parents and godparents renew their Baptismal Promises, it is finally time for the central aspect of the Sacrament. Picture yourself at this point. Do you imagine yourself being immersed in the water, or do you imagine the water being poured over your head?

The priest says the name of the candidate and immerses him or her in water three times or pours water on his or her head three times while saying these

© Francesco Maria Cura'

Have you ever seen Baptism by immersion? Immersion is a rich sign of dying to sin and rising to new life.

# Catholic Connection

## The Trinity

Christians are baptized in the name of the Father, and of the Son, and of the Holy Spirit. This means we are baptized in the name of the one God, who has made himself known to us in the three divine Persons of the Trinity: the Father, the Son, and the Holy Spirit. The Trinity is the central mystery of our faith. We say it's a mystery because our brains cannot completely understand the Trinity. Though we can know a lot about God through reason, we have to depend on our faith in God, who has made himself known to us through Revelation.

The three Persons are all one God, one divine being. They are distinct Persons, but are completely in union with one another. This communion means that the work they do is always the accomplishment of all three Persons. However, some of God's works are more strongly associated with a particular one.

The Father is the first Person of the Trinity. We often think of God the Father as the Creator. This is true, but remember it is also true that the Son and the Holy Spirit created the world. Like a parent, the Father is the source from which life comes. It is natural to have the Father in our minds when we think of Creation.

Jesus Christ is the second Person of the Trinity. He is the Savior. This title helps us to recognize all he did for the sake of our salvation. We cannot forget, though, that the Father and the Holy Spirit save us too.

The Holy Spirit, the third Person of the Trinity, inspires and guides us, and makes our lives holy. We recognize that many gifts are given to us by the Holy Spirit, but these gifts are truly given by the Father and the Son too.

Even though each Person of the Trinity is distinct, it is one God who creates, and saves, and makes us holy. One God in three Persons—it's as simple, and as complicated, as that!

words: "I baptize you in the name of the Father, and of the Son, and of the Holy Spirit." The child is baptized in the name of the Trinity.

Whether a candidate is immersed or whether the water is poured, the water ritual is a sacramental sign of God's action. It is important to understand what God does for us through Baptism:

- God cleanses us and washes away Original Sin and all personal sin if we are old enough to have committed any.
- God brings us new life in Christ and makes us adopted children of the Father.
- God helps us to see the world as filled with goodness.
- God makes us brothers and sisters of Christ.
- God helps us to see ourselves as filled with the Holy Spirit.
- God incorporates us into the Church, the Body of Christ.

- God makes us sharers in the priesthood of Christ, which means we are people who, through Christ, know the Father and help others know him too.

You can see why the Church uses water, a symbol of life and death, in Baptism. Baptismal waters cleanse us and bring us new life, but they also bring an end to our old selves and to sin.

## More Oil

Yes, more oil. After Baptism children are anointed on the top of the head with a sacred oil called Chrism. It is perfumed olive oil that has been consecrated by the bishop. (It is used in Confirmation and the Sacrament of Holy Orders too.) At Baptism the anointing with Sacred Chrism signifies that the one who has been baptized has received the gift of the Holy Spirit.

© Bill Wittman

At your Baptism you were anointed with Sacred Chrism and received the Holy Spirit. How has the Holy Spirit been active in your life since the day of your Baptism?

# Jesus Connection

## Priest, Prophet, King

Through Baptism you were incorporated into Christ's mission as priest, prophet, and king. Let's consider what it means to share in this mission:

**Priest.** We are priestly when our lives are marked by holiness. This means being open to the Holy Spirit in all we do. This includes in our family lives, in our school-work, in our free time, in our care of our-selves and others, and even in our prayer, both on our own and with others, such as at Mass.

**Prophet.** We are prophetic when we announce the Good News of Jesus Christ. This means striving to grow in our faith and being willing to share it with others through actions and words.

**King.** Jesus fulfilled his kingly role by being a leader who served others. We participate in this mission when we use our gifts to help people who are in need.

The words the priest speaks just before the anointing express its significance:

God the Father of our Lord Jesus Christ
has freed you from sin,
given you a new birth
by water and the Holy Spirit,
and welcomed you into his holy people.

He now anoints you with the chrism of salvation,
As Christ was anointed Priest, Prophet, and King,
so may you live always as members of his body,
sharing everlasting life.

*(Rite of Baptism for Children*, number 62)

The title Christ means "anointed one." This anointing shows that the newly baptized child is a member of the Body of Christ and has a new name—Christian.

## Giving the White Garment

Remember your First Communion dress, girls? Boys, you may have worn a nice, white shirt at your First Communion. Brides often wear white. Girls who celebrate Quinceañera when they turn fifteen often wear white too. Can you think of other times when the color white is used or preferred?

The newly baptized receive a white garment to symbolize newness of life. Do you know what your white garment looked like?

Children wear white garments at Baptism. You may have arrived for your Baptism already dressed in a special white gown or outfit. Or, if you were baptized by immersion, you were most likely dressed in white after being dried off. Regardless of when you were clothed, the white color is significant. Why white? What do you think about when you think of the color white? A new, untouched snowfall? clean, crisp sheets or towels? a newborn fluffy lamb?

White symbolizes purity and cleanliness. The white garment you wore at your Baptism was a sign of your new life in Christ. In Baptism you were washed clean and made new.

## The Light of Christ at Baptism

What do you think of when you think of light? Brightness and warmth? A candle or flashlight can light your way on a dark

In Baptism I was washed clean
and made a new creation.
I am thankful God, to you,
and to those who brought
me to the waters of Baptism.
Help me to live as one of
your children. Help me to
live as a child of the light.
I pray this prayer in your
name; in the name of the
Father, and of the Son, and
of the Holy Spirit.
Amen.

# My Mission

## Spread the Light of Christ

You received the light of Christ at your Baptism. This light is meant to be spread throughout the world. Name three specific ways you can spread the light of Christ to others.

1.

2.

3.

night. A fire in the fireplace can change a cold and drafty room into a warm and cozy room. Even a small flame can pierce the darkness.

In Baptism a lighted candle is the symbol for the light of Christ. The light of Christ shatters the darkness of sin and death. This light burns in your heart. Christ burns in your heart. The light of Christ will guide you throughout your life.

You received the light of Christ at your Baptism. To symbolize this, someone from your family lit a small baptismal candle from

© Bill Wittman

The small, white candle that you received at Baptism was lit from the Paschal candle. The Paschal candle is a symbol of Christ. In what ways does the light of Christ guide your daily path?

the big Easter candle, which is also called the Paschal candle. The priest explained that the light was being entrusted to the parents and godparents to be kept burning brightly, and he prayed that the flame of faith would be kept alive in your heart.

How is the light of Christ manifested in your life right now? Think of the bright spots in your life that indicate the light of Christ is burning. Do any of these examples fit: hanging out with your friends? doing well at your recital or game? having dinner at Grandma's? spending one-on-one time with Dad? treating others with kindness?

## Reborn in Baptism

On the day of your Baptism, you were reborn as a child of God and made a member of the Church. Baptism was the beginning of your new life in Christ. At the end of the celebration of your Baptism, the priest sent you forth to grow as a child of God and a member of the Church. The pathway to salvation was opened up for you since Baptism is necessary for salvation.

Confirmation is an important step in continuing your growth as a Catholic and a member of the Church. Through Confirmation you will receive the fullness of the Holy Spirit, which will deepen the life of faith that began at Baptism.

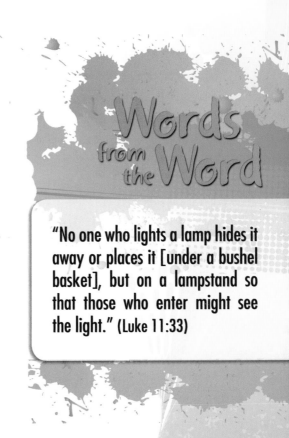

Words from the Word

"No one who lights a lamp hides it away or places it [under a bushel basket], but on a lampstand so that those who enter might see the light." (Luke 11:33)

# A Letter to My Godparents

Your godparents helped your parents bring you to Baptism. Do you know your godparents? Some people know their godparents very well. Others may not know their godparents at all. You may only have one godparent. What would you like to say to your godparent or godparents? Use the space provided to record your thoughts. Consider including reflections about your faith.

# 3 Renewing Baptismal Promises

I promise I won't tell. You can trust me . . . I promise! I promise to do my homework after one more game! I promise I'm not mad at you. I promise we'll go to sleep by 1:00 a.m. I promise I'll try harder. . . . How often do you make promises like these? They may seem sort of common, but promises are really important, and some are more important than others.

© Steve Hix/Somos Images/Corbis

Keeping a friend's secret is really important. Your friend trusts you, and you must respect that trust. But sometimes telling an adult someone's secret is necessary, like when a person's safety and well-being are at stake. However, breaking your promise and telling a friend's secret for no good reason is just plain wrong. You know the difference.

Other promises aren't quite so weighty. I promise to wear the sweater Grandma made me. I promise to eat my vegetables while I'm at camp. Promises like these

Some promises are made in a light-hearted way. Other promises are solemn commitments. How important is giving your word to a friend? How important are Baptismal Promises?

aren't quite as significant—although you do have to admit that you've given your word, no matter how big the promise.

All in all, a promise is important because we're giving a type of guarantee that we'll do what we say. A promise is a solemn agreement. If we break the agreement, we sometimes hurt someone. We may become untrustworthy. Nobody wants that. We all want others to trust us. We want to be taken at our word. We want our promises to mean something. And they do. Our promises mean a lot!

## Baptismal Promises

Did you know there are promises made at Baptism, even when those being baptized are babies? The parents and godparents promise to reject sin and to believe in God—Father, Son, and Holy Spirit. If you were baptized as a baby, you were certainly too young to make promises. Sometimes this part of the Baptism ritual is explained by saying that your parents and godparents made the Baptismal Promises for you. Well, that's not *exactly* what happens. No one makes any promises *for* the baby. But, if you were a baby, then who made promises for whom? Let's see.

## Who Made Promises for Whom?

How would you feel if someone else made a promise for you? What if your dad said to a coach, "I promise that Sydney will work hard and be the best player on the team." Or what if your aunt said, "I promise that Jack will do the dishes every night." How would that work? It doesn't make much sense, does it?

At the Baptism of young children, parents and godparents make promises. They answer questions *for themselves* about their own faith.

By bringing children to the Catholic Church to be baptized, parents and godparents make a promise to raise those children in the Catholic faith. So during the celebration of Baptism, the priest asks them to profess or state what they believe. It's not that the parents and godparents speak for their children; rather, they give voice to the faith of the Church in which their children are being baptized.

Throughout this chapter, we are going to look at the promises that parents and godparents make at Baptism and that you will renew at Confirmation. The questions are very similar, whether it's Baptism or Confirmation.

## The Promises Made at Baptism

Actually, what we call Baptismal Promises aren't exactly like the promises we talked about at the beginning of the chapter. You don't say, "I promise to do this" or "I promise not to do that." Baptismal Promises are really questions and answers about what we believe. The

Your parents and godparents guide you in the Catholic way of life. The Church helps them in their role.

© Silvia Jansen/istockphoto.com

## Words from the Word

"Children, let no one deceive you. The person who acts in righteousness is righteous, just as he is righteous. Whoever sins belongs to the devil, because the devil has sinned from the beginning. Indeed, the Son of God was revealed to destroy the works of the devil." (1 John 3:7–8)

priest asks the parents and godparents several questions about sin and about God. The questions fall into two groups of three questions each:

1. **Renunciation of sin.** The first set of three questions is about rejecting sin. The priest asks the parents and godparents if they reject Satan and all sin. Of course, they say, "I do."

2. **Profession of faith.** The second set of three questions is about what we believe. Again the priest asks the parents and godparents questions about the Father, Jesus Christ, the Holy Spirit, the Church, saints, sins, and Heaven. And, again, they say, "I do."

It is helpful to notice a couple things here:

- The parents and godparents say, "*I do.*" They do not say, "Yes, she does believe, but she is just too little to speak for herself, so I'm speaking for her." Your parents and godparents testify to their *own* faith.

- The questions we're talking about here are like the questions you will be asked during the celebration of the Sacrament of Confirmation. But at Confirmation, the renunciation of sin is covered in one question, and the profession of faith is covered in four questions (see "Renewal of Baptismal Promises" in appendix A).

# Catholic Connection

## Satan and Evil

Satan is one of God's creatures. He is a good angel gone bad. The *Catechism of the Catholic Church (CCC)* refers to Satan as a seductive voice and describes him as a fallen angel who is pure spirit (see numbers 391, 395). Satan had the original holiness that all God's creatures had, but then by his own free choice he rejected God.

Satan is part of the explanation of why evil exists in the world. Satan is working in the world against God. Some people freely make evil choices. Every human being has free will, and some reject God. Further, some choices come together in ways that make an entire system evil. For example, the discrimination against blacks in South Africa, under a system called apartheid, denied the God-given dignity of a large number of people and led to great suffering. Eventually, apartheid was dismantled.

Satan cannot stand in the way of God's will. And we know, with 100 percent certainty, that God's power and love are greater than Satan.

© Richard Nebesky/Robert Harding World Imagery/Corbis

This memorial shows children from the village of Lidice, Czech Republic sent to a concentration camp by the Nazis. They were victims of horrible evil. Although evil is very real, God always prevails.

## Renouncing Sin at Confirmation

Would you agree that there is evil in the world? Just think about the terrorist attacks of 9-11. We ask ourselves, "What makes people do such horrible things?" There are a lot of complicated reasons behind why those attacks occurred. One of the reasons is that evil exists in our world. People do evil things and get caught up in evil systems. The First Letter of John makes reference to "the power of the evil one" (5:19). Another name for the Evil One is Satan. (See "Catholic Connection" sidebar on page 45 for more on Satan.)

You would probably also agree that there is sin in the world. Some sins are evil and very serious, while other sins are less serious. Sin is anything we say, do, or desire that goes against God's law. When we sin we act in a way that contradicts reason. We disobey God and fail to follow Christ's example. Serious sins are called mortal sins. A mortal sin is something we purposely choose that goes so seriously against God's will that it completely separates us from God. A mortal sin requires that we know we are committing serious sin and that we freely choose to do it. We cannot commit a mortal sin by accident or if someone is forcing us to do it. It is called mortal because separation from God leads to eternal death. It destroys our love for God and others and makes eternal happiness with God impossible. Venial sins are less serious sins. They weaken our relationships with God and others and hurt our personal character. When you renew your Baptismal Promises at Confirmation, you will be renouncing sins of all kinds.

The bishop asks the candidates the following question: "Do you renounce Satan, and all his works and empty promises?" (*Order of Confirmation*, number 23). The answer "I do" is called a renunciation, but what does it mean?

## What Does *Renounce* Mean?

Renounce drugs! Renounce bullying! Renounce cigarettes! Renounce alcohol! These are all messages you've probably heard in health class at school. When we renounce something, we reject it—definitely! To renounce something is to officially or formally give it up. It means saying no, without wavering.

To say no to Satan, his works, and his empty promises means to say no to sin and to reject all that is evil. By saying no to Satan, you are saying you will do your best not to sin. Of course, there will be times in your life when you do sin, but you are promising to do your best to reject sin. In fact, you are rejecting a way of life that follows Satan and choosing a life of good that follows Christ. You are rejecting a way of life that is contrary to God's law. You are choosing a way of life that follows God's will.

Let's consider some examples of what you are rejecting when you "renounce Satan, and all his works and empty promises" (*Order of Confirmation*, number 23). An empty promise of Satan's might be something like this: "If you wear cool clothes and own the latest technological gadgets, then you are more important

You are the Almighty One,
 Creator of Heaven and earth.
I give you thanks and praise
 for your Son, Jesus Christ,
 whom you sent to save us.
I ask for your Holy Spirit
 to be with me as I prepare
 for Confirmation.
I pray that the Spirit will teach
 me the things I need to know,
 not just about Confirmation,
 but about your love for
 me and all of the world.
Help me to reject the Evil
 One and to always rely
 on your goodness.
I ask this through Christ
 our Lord.
Amen.

than others who don't." If people get caught up in this kind of thinking, and especially if they make decisions about how to treat people based on it, then they have given in to an empty promise.

Material things are not evil, but when people place too much value on possessions, it can lead to a rejection of the God-given dignity that every person has. Rejecting Satan means saying no to this and to other ways of thinking and acting that are sinful.

The renunciation at Confirmation includes Satan's. works as well as promises. Here are some examples of works to reject:

- bullying others
- being selfish and unkind
- cheating on schoolwork or lying
- using tobacco, illegal drugs, and alcohol
- behaving inappropriately and using inappropriate language

When you say no to things like these, you are rejecting Satan.

## Profession of Faith at Confirmation

Once you have stated your rejection of Satan, the Church asks you to profess, or state publicly, what it is you believe. All this echoes those promises made at Baptism by your parents and godparents. Amazingly, these questions go back way beyond

© Radius Images/Corbis

Is gossip a sin? Is talking behind someone's back one of the "works of Satan"? When you resist sinful actions, you reject the works of Satan. You say no to sin and evil.

## Creeds

A creed is a statement of beliefs. The word *creed* is based on the Latin word *credo*, which means "I believe."

As Catholics we express our beliefs by answering questions and by making statements. When we answer questions, as in Confirmation, we are using a type of creedal expression that can be called interrogatory (think about what happens during an interrogation). Creedal statements, such as the Nicene Creed and the Apostles' Creed, can be called declarative (think about the manner of speech used when you declare something).

The Q-and-A type of profession was part of ancient Baptisms. In the earliest days of the Church, most of the people seeking Baptism were adults, so they answered for themselves. Unlike babies, adults seeking Baptism are consciously turning away from an old life. This was the reason for the inclusion of the renunciation of sin before the profession. Sometimes in the early Church, as a sign of conversion (meaning "a change of heart"), the candidates faced west (associated with darkness and the devil) to renounce sin, and then they turned away from the devil and faced east (associated with light) to affirm their Christian beliefs.

Declarative creeds also have a long history in the Church. Two of the most important creeds are the Apostles' Creed and the Nicene Creed. The Apostles' Creed is regarded as a faithful summary of the Apostles' beliefs. It is authoritative because it was the creed for the ancient Church of Rome. The Nicene Creed is authoritative because it was officially approved by the Church in the fourth century. At Sunday Mass, Catholics profess belief by reciting the Nicene Creed together. "To say the Credo with faith is to enter into communion with God, Father, Son, and Holy Spirit, and also with the whole Church" (CCC, number 197).

# Questions at Confirmation

The Church sometimes expresses beliefs through stained-glass artwork. What belief is expressed here?

© Bill Wittman

| Profession of Faith | Apostles' Creed |
|---|---|
| Do you believe in God, the Father almighty, Creator of heaven and earth? | I believe in God, the Father almighty, Creator of heaven and earth, |
| Do you believe in Jesus Christ, his only Son, our Lord, who was born of the Virgin Mary, suffered death and was buried, rose again from the dead and is seated at the right hand of the Father? | and in Jesus Christ, his only Son, our Lord, who was conceived by the Holy Spirit, born of the Virgin Mary, suffered under Pontius Pilate, was crucified, died and was buried; he descended into hell; on the third day he rose again from the dead; he ascended into heaven, and is seated at the right hand of God the Father almighty; from there he will come to judge the living and the dead. |
| Do you believe in the Holy Spirit, the Lord, the giver of life, who today through the Sacrament of Confirmation is given to you in a special way just as he was given to the Apostles on the day of Pentecost? Do you believe in the holy Catholic Church, the communion of saints, the forgiveness of sins, the resurrection of the body, and life everlasting? (Order of Confirmation, 23) | I believe in the Holy Spirit, the holy catholic Church, the communion of saints, the forgiveness of sins, the resurrection of the body, and life everlasting. Amen. |

your Baptism—to Baptisms celebrated during the earliest days of the Church (see the "Did You Know?" sidebar on page 49).

The questions ask if you believe what the Church believes. They are very similar to the Church's two most important creeds, the Apostles' Creed and the Nicene Creed. The questions at Confirmation summarize the same central beliefs as the creeds, but they do so in the form of questions.

Take a look at the "Questions at Confirmation" sidebar on page 50. Notice how the questions the bishop asks you at Confirmation correspond to the three parts of the Apostles' Creed. Notice also that each of the three parts relates to one Person of the Trinity. Both the Apostles' Creed and the Profession of Faith questions reflect our central belief that God is Father, Son, and Holy Spirit. (To compare the Profession of the Faith questions with the Nicene Creed, read through the Nicene Creed in appendix A.)

## Make It Public, Make It Personal

You may have renewed your Baptismal Promises several times before coming to the Sacrament of Confirmation. If you've been to the Easter Vigil on Holy Saturday, then you've renewed them. If you've been to a baby's Baptism, the celebrant may have had you join with parents and godparents in renewing your promises.

## Right from the Rite

"This is our faith. This is the faith of the Church. We are proud to profess it in Christ Jesus our Lord." (*Order of Confirmation*, number 23)

## Jesus Connection

# Jesus = God Saves

You were baptized in the name of the Father, Son, and Holy Spirit. The name of the Son is Jesus, but did you know that the name Jesus in Hebrew means "God saves"? The name Jesus tells us who he is and what he does. He is Jesus of Nazareth, the Son of God, and his mission is to save us. Through Jesus' suffering, death, and Resurrection, the sins of all humanity were taken away. Jesus died for our sins that we might have life everlasting. His death and Resurrection accomplished our salvation. Because he took on the sins of the world, we can enjoy eternal life.

In Baptism we celebrate the dying of our old selves to sin and the rising of our new lives in Jesus Christ. We are joined to Jesus' death and Resurrection. In Jesus, "God saves."

In the Sacrament of Confirmation, the focus will be on *you*, the Confirmation candidate. Although the bishop will be talking to a whole group when he asks the questions, imagine he is looking right at you! And you will answer, "I do." Notice it's not a group answer; it's not "We do." You are answering as an individual person of faith.

The Church is asking you to make a personal and public proclamation of your faith just before being confirmed. By stating what you believe, you are making a statement about how you intend to live your life as a follower of Christ.

## Renewing Promises

Have you ever renewed a library card or a membership to a gym or recreation center? Have you heard your mom or dad talk about renewing a driver's license? Maybe you know adults who have renewed their wedding vows. Perhaps you've repeated a promise you made to a friend.

When you renew something, you are saying yes again. You are saying, "I still want to do this." When you renew Baptismal Promises, you are saying things like, "I want to keep being a Catholic," "I reject sinful choices," and "I want to live as a disciple of Jesus Christ."

These are the promises you renew for yourself at Confirmation. It's about how you want to live your whole life. When you renew or restate your promises publicly, your resolve to do what you say you want to do grows stronger.

## Living the Promises

The promises you renew during the Sacrament of Confirmation are big. You are promising to live as one who follows Christ. You are promising to live as a believer, a believer in God—the Father, Son, and Holy Spirit. That's a really important promise. It's like when you give your word to your grandmother. It's like when you promise a best friend that she or he can depend on you. It's like when you promise a parent that you will definitely be there to take care of your little brother. Sometimes it's hard for us to fulfill all the promises associated with Christian living. But we're not doing it on our own. The Holy Spirit is with us and makes it possible for us to live the promise.

# My Mission

## To Live the Promise

The Renewal of Baptismal Promises involves promising to reject sin and to follow Christ. How do you already live out this promise? In the space below, write or draw examples of how you reject or say no to sin.

Write or draw examples of how you follow or say yes to Christ.

## Proud to Profess

After you renew your Baptismal Promises at Confirmation, the bishop says: "This is the faith of the Church. We are proud to profess it in Christ Jesus our Lord." What about your faith makes you proud or happy?

# 4 The Laying On of Hands

They had been building this rocket for three weeks. It counted for most of their grade in technology class. The time for launching had come. Ben pulled back the enormous rubber band, and Michael placed the rocket in the holder. Blast off! The rocket sailed to the top of the light post and landed all the way over on the playground. The whole class burst into cheers! Ben and Michael turned to each other with arms extended, fists jutting outward in knuckles—double knuckles. This was definitely double knuckles.

Hand gestures convey a lot of meaning. Knuckles mean: "Way to go. Good job. Nicely done." Your parents may still do the high five. It means the same thing. A parent pats you on the back after a well-played game: "Good effort." A teacher may put up a hand to signal stop, just as you are about to explain why you don't

When is the last time you used this gesture or saw someone else use it? What did it mean to you? to the other person?

have your homework. That means: "I don't want to hear it." What other hand gestures can you think of? (Yes, there are lots of rude, inappropriate gestures too, but let's stick to the positive ones.)

## It's in the Hands

Hand gestures communicate a great deal of meaning because our hands are central to all we do: working, cooking, writing, painting, drawing, playing games, playing instruments, playing sports, bathing, healing, touching, hugging, and so on.

Much can be expressed in just a simple touch of the hand. A boy and girl holding hands means they like each other. Grandpa's wrinkled hand placed tenderly on top of yours means he loves you. Mom's hard-working hands placed sweetly on your cheeks means she is proud of you. A doctor's gentle hand

on your broken wrist means you'll be healed soon. Dad's sturdy hand squeezing your hand means, "I know you can you do it!"

(In addition, we must say something difficult directly. There is such a thing as a bad touch. A person's hands can cause great harm. Hands can be used to hurt, kill, and destroy people. Touch can be used inappropriately. Tragically, children can be the victims of sexually bad touching. If you know someone who is a victim, or if you want to talk more about this topic, talk to your teacher, a parent, or another adult you trust.)

There is something about physical touch that is significant. The human touch makes us feel connected to people. Under positive circumstances, human touch can convey warmth, goodness, unity, concern, power, healing, and even love.

© Klaus Tiedge/Corbis

You can show your love, compassion, and concern without saying a word — just use your hands. Appropriate and loving touch is important in human relationships.

## The Hands of God

What is your favorite creation from art class? The flower picture or clay animal you made in second grade? Has a parent ever saved one of your childhood creations just because you made it with your own hands?

God made all of creation "with his own hands"[1] (*Catechism of the Catholic Church* [CCC], number 704). This quotation is from Saint Irenaeus, who calls the Son and the Spirit the hands of God. They are inseparable from the Father. Whenever God sends the Son, he sends the Holy Spirit too. Their mission is inseparable. Jesus is the one who was seen walking on earth. But the Spirit was there. Jesus is the one who was healing the sick, feeding the hungry, and raising the dead. But it was also the Spirit. The "hands" can never be separated from one another or from the Father who sent them.

The images of Word and Breath also express the unity of the three Persons of the Trinity. The Father sends his Word (Jesus Christ), but he also always sends his Breath (the Holy Spirit) at the same time.

The Word spoken and the Breath that breathes the words cannot be separated. And it is the Father who does the speaking. These images help us to understand that the Father, Son, and Holy Spirit are one God in three persons.

© Peter Finger/Corbis

God is the potter and we are the clay. This image from Jeremiah leads us to imagine that God's hands form us. God creates and fashions all creation. What special characteristic or gift did God form in you?

## Jesus' Healing Hand

Jesus gave sight to those who could not see and hearing to those with deafness. He gave voice to those who were mute and healed the bodies of those who could not walk. He drove out demons from those possessed by the devil. He raised the dead. And he often used his hands to do it!

Interestingly, the Scriptures often describe Jesus' touching people when he heals them (see Matthew 8:3, Mark 7:32–33). We also hear of Jesus' taking a sick person by the hand when he heals him or her (see Mark 1:31, 5:41). This points out how personally connected Jesus was with the people he healed. Touch is a very personal and intimate gesture.

Jesus' healing hand showed that Jesus had divine power. Jesus' ability to heal was a sign of his divinity. It is one of the signs that he is truly the Son of God.

## The Power of Hands

In the Scriptures, human hands and the human touch express the power of God's love for us. Let's look at a few stories from the Bible to see the meaning and power found in hands.

A great Old Testament story includes the hand of the Lord and the hand of Moses. God tells Moses, "The Egyptians shall know that I am the Lord, when I stretch out my hand against Egypt and bring the Israelites out from among them" (Exodus 7:5, NRSV). Then, throughout the conflict with Pharaoh, Moses raises his hand to bring plagues upon Egypt. Finally: "Moses stretched out his hand over the sea, and the Lord swept the sea with a strong east wind throughout the night and so turned it into dry land. . . . [T]he Israelites marched into the midst of the sea on dry land" (14:21–22). Moses' hand is a sign of God's power and glory.

Hands convey God's power in the New Testament also, but in a different way. In the New Testament, we see Jesus and the Apostles laying hands on people as signs of healing and at times of initiation into the Church. The laying on of hands or the imposition of hands

© PoodlesRock/Corbis

Notice the interaction between Jesus and the sick girl. What does she see in Jesus' face as he reaches out to her?

# Many Symbols of the Holy Spirit

We use a variety of signs and symbols in addition to the laying on of hands to express the presence and power of the Holy Spirit. Here are several:

**Breath.** The word *Spirit* in Hebrew is *ruah*. It means "breath or air or wind." We often think of the Spirit as wind because both the Spirit and wind are invisible but forceful. The Holy Spirit was present at creation when "a wind from God swept over the face of the waters" (Genesis 1:2, NRSV).

**Advocate.** Jesus uses the title Advocate for the Holy Spirit: "I will ask the Father, and he will give you another Advocate, to be with you forever" (John 14:16, NRSV). *Advocate* is a translation of the Greek word *paraclete*. An advocate is someone who stands by another and supports her or him. Here is an example: "I am an advocate for children who are abused." Some Bibles translate *advocate* as *helper*.

**Fire.** Fire is a symbol of the Holy Spirit because, like fire, the Holy Spirit has the power to transform.

**Water.** In John's Gospel, Jesus says, "Let anyone who thirsts come to me and drink. Whoever believes in me, as scripture says: 'Rivers of living water will flow from within him'" (John 7:37–38). When Jesus refers to living water, he is speaking about the Holy Spirit.

**Dove.** When Jesus came up out of the water after being baptized, the Spirit of God descended upon him "like a dove" (Matthew 3:16). Do you ever see the Holy Spirit depicted as a dove in stained-glass windows, in religious paintings, on cards, on posters, or in books?

**Anointing.** Anointing with oil is a sign of the Holy Spirit's being poured out upon a person.

©Bill Wittman

The fire at the Easter Vigil shatters darkness and points to the radiance of Christ.

# My Mission

## Use Your Hands

As the bishop lays hands upon you in Confirmation, he will pray that you will be filled with the Holy Spirit. Your mission is to use your hands and your whole self to cooperate with the work of the Spirit. In the space below, list two things you have done or can do today to show that the Holy Spirit already lives in you.

is an ancient gesture associated with the coming of the Holy Spirit. Let's look at some ways the laying on of hands is used in the New Testament.

In the New Testament, Jesus' hands bring healing power to others. Jesus uses his hands to touch and heal. We see the tenderness of the human touch reflected in Jesus' ministry. In Matthew's Gospel, a leper says to Jesus, "'Lord, if you choose, you can make me clean'" (8:2, NRSV). Jesus stretches out his hand and touches the leper, saying: "'I do choose. Be made clean!'" (8:3, NRSV). The Gospel of Mark mentions that Jesus "laid his hands on a few sick people and cured them" (6:5, NRSV). By laying his hands on the man's eyes, Jesus healed a man who was blind (see 8:23–25). Also, Jesus took little children up in his arms and "laid his hands on them, and blessed them" (10:16, NRSV). When Jesus sent the Apostles out to spread the Good News, he said that those who believe "will lay their hands on the sick, and they will recover" (16:18, NRSV).

The laying on of hands is also a sign of the coming of the Holy Spirit apart from physical healing. The Gospel of John describes the Spirit coming upon the disciples. They were gathered together in a locked room after Jesus' Resurrection when Jesus appeared to them and said: "'Peace be with you. As the Father has sent me, so I send you.' And when he had said this, he breathed on them and said to them, 'Receive the holy Spirit'" (20:21–22). After receiving the Holy Spirit, the disciples began to more actively spread the Good News of Jesus. They baptized many believers and laid hands on them. The laying on of hands indicated the coming of the Holy Spirit. Here are two examples:

**Peter and John in Samaria.** The people of Samaria who had accepted the Word of God were baptized in the name of the Lord Jesus. After they were baptized, Peter and John "laid hands on them and they received the holy Spirit" (Acts of the Apostles 8:17).

**Paul in Ephesus.** While the Apostle Paul was in the city of Ephesus, some people were baptized in the name of the Lord Jesus. Then, "when Paul laid [his] hands on them, the holy Spirit came upon them" (Acts of the Apostles 19:6).

In both examples, the laying on of hands comes after Baptism, and it's specifically linked to the coming of the Holy Spirit. Let's look further at this gesture of laying on of hands and its role in Confirmation.

At Pentecost the Holy Spirit came upon the disciples and appeared as tongues of fire. In what way is the Spirit present in your life? How do you know?

## Laying On of Hands in the Sacrament of Confirmation

The Church continues to use the ancient gesture of laying on of hands to signify the gift of the Holy Spirit. The gesture is an important aspect of Confirmation. The bishop will lay hands on you and all the candidates by extending his hands over everyone. He will ask the Father to pour out the Holy Spirit so that you will be strengthened with the Spirit's gifts. You will be anointed so that you will become more like Christ. As the bishop extends his hands, he will pray that God will fill you with the Gifts of the Holy Spirit. (We will explore the Gifts of the Holy Spirit in chapter 5 and anointing in chapter 6.)

The bishop's laying on of hands communicates a great deal of meaning. Remember the examples of hand gestures at the beginning of this chapter? Recall how much care, concern, love, pride, healing, and strength can be packed into a single touch of a hand. Remember how God's power flowed through Moses' hand, Jesus' hands possessed divine power for healing and blessing, and the Apostles' hands signified the coming of the Spirit. So too the bishop's hand gesture in Confirmation is associated with the very real presence and power of the Holy Spirit. The bishop's hand doesn't control the Spirit, but it is a sign of what the Spirit is doing.

Here is a really important point about laying on of hands and the Holy Spirit to keep in mind. The Holy Spirit comes upon the baptized. The outpouring of the Holy Spirit in Confirmation doesn't mean that the Spirit was missing at Baptism. But the laying on of hands *after* Baptism gives special attention to the presence of the Holy Spirit. In Baptism the Holy Spirit takes away sin and makes us a new creation. In Confirmation the Holy Spirit strengthens us and makes us more like Jesus Christ.

What we need to remember in all of this is that the laying on of hands is associated with the Holy Spirit's presence and that a special outpouring of the Holy Spirit takes place at Confirmation.

## A Little History

We know from the descriptions in the Acts of the Apostles and from early Church writings that after a person was baptized, there was a laying on of hands. We also know that there was an anointing after Baptism. Finally, the new Christian received the Eucharist for the first time. The celebrations of Baptism, Confirmation, and the Eucharist were carried out in the same liturgy. The Eucharist was, and still is, the high point of Christian initiation. In fact, the Eucharist is the high point of the entire Christian life. (We'll talk more about the Eucharist in chapter 7.)

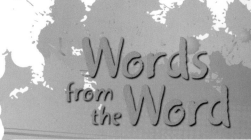

## Words from the Word

"Let us leave behind the basic teaching about Christ and advance to maturity, without laying the foundation all over again: repentance from dead works and faith in God, instruction about baptisms and laying on of hands, resurrection of the dead and eternal judgment." (Hebrews 6:1–2)

**Dear God**

You sent your Holy Spirit upon
the disciples on Pentecost.
You gave me that same Holy
Spirit at my Baptism.
I pray that the Spirit will guide
my hands to do good and
my feet to follow in the ways
of your Son, Jesus Christ.
Help me also to speak with
the breath of the
Holy Spirit.
I pray this prayer in the
name of your Son,
Jesus, who lives and reigns
forever and ever.
Amen.

Let's put together what we learned in the last chapter about Baptismal Promises with what we have learned in this chapter. Try to picture what an ancient baptismal ceremony might have looked like:

The candidates stood near a large pool or baptismal font waiting for Baptism. (Sometimes Baptisms took place in a baptistery, outside of the church, and then the newly baptized came into the church for Confirmation and the Eucharist.) They faced west and renounced Satan. Then they turned and faced east and made the profession of faith. Then the candidates undressed and were anointed with oil. Baptism by immersion followed. Then the candidates came out of the water, got dressed in white garments, and went to the main area of the church. The bishop laid hands on them, anointed them, and prayed for them. This was followed by the Eucharist.

© Bill Wittman

Look how deep this ancient baptismal font is. The candidate walked down the steps, was baptized, then walked out the other side and into the church to be anointed by the bishop.

This is just a rough sketch of what Baptism, Confirmation, and the Eucharist may have looked like in the early Christian centuries. It may have looked a little different from place to place, but the essential elements and the meaning would have been the same.

As time went on, the Church grew larger and more people were being initiated. It wasn't possible for bishops to baptize and anoint everyone. Two different practices emerged as a result. In the Churches in the West, the bishop continued to confirm the baptized. The West focused on the connection of the bishops to Jesus' Apostles. The bishops are successors to the Apostles, so every bishop has a special connection directly to Jesus. (See chapter 6 for more on bishops as successors to the Apostles.) To keep the strong connection between the bishop and Jesus, Western Churches delayed Confirmation until a point in time when the bishop could do the anointing. This practice of separating Confirmation from Baptism continues in the West today.

The Churches in the East kept the celebrations of Baptism and Confirmation together. The connection to the Apostles was important, but for them the connection was less in the presence of the bishop and more in the oil consecrated by the bishop. Whether or not the bishop was present, Eastern Churches continued to baptize and confirm in the same liturgy as long as they had oil

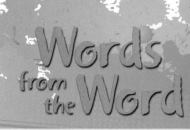

## Words from the Word

"While they were worshiping the Lord and fasting, the holy Spirit said, 'Set apart for me Barnabas and Saul for the work to which I have called them.' Then, completing their fasting and prayer, they laid hands on them and sent them off." (Acts of the Apostles 13:2–3)

consecrated by the bishop (called Sacred Chrism). Confirmation was then immediately followed by the Eucharist. This practice, which continues in the East today, clearly shows the close connection and unity among the three Sacraments of Christian Initiation—Baptism, Confirmation, and the Eucharist.

Whether Confirmation comes right after Baptism or years later, and whether we recall ancient practice or focus on the celebration of Sacraments today, the gesture of laying on of hands signifies the outpouring of the Holy Spirit.

## Your Hands Today

The next time you raise your hand to answer a question or bump fists with someone or pat someone on the back, think about the significance of hands. They are full of meaning. And remember that your hands and your whole person are filled with the Holy Spirit.

# A Helping Hand

We've talked a lot about a hand gesture being a symbol of the outpouring of the Holy Spirit. And we've talked a lot about what hands can do. Name a time when another person's hand was a sign of support and help for you. Maybe a friend put a hand on your shoulder when you were upset. Or maybe your dad held your hand when you were afraid you'd get some bad news. Describe how this support or help was a sign of the Holy Spirit.

# 5 The Gifts of the Holy Spirit

Why was everything going wrong in his life? None of his friends were in any of his classes. He'd made the B team in basketball. He was getting a D in science. And now he'd just found out his dad was sick. It might even be cancer. Brandon felt awful, hopelessly awful. There was nothing anyone could do to help him.

But what about Mrs. Carter, his English teacher? She always said she was there to help kids with whatever they needed. She'd understand. Maybe he could talk to her. Yes, he'd try it. He'd look for Mrs. Carter in the gym after school today. She was always there.

Can you name some of the people who help and guide you? The Holy Spirit is also a helper and guide.

© Gabe Palmer/Corbis

Sure enough, Mrs. Carter was a big help to Brandon. They actually talked for a long time. In fact, now they talked just about every day. Somehow Mrs. Carter knew just what to say. Somehow things were better. Somehow even Brandon's jump shot was getting better!

Mrs. Carter helped Brandon through a difficult time. She was there for him. Sometimes she didn't even really say anything, but Brandon knew she was there if he needed her. Mrs. Carter had been a helper and guide through those tough times. Brandon didn't always know exactly what it was she had done for him, but he knew she had helped. Mrs. Carter comforted Brandon, made him feel stronger and more self-assured.

## Helper and Guide

People who help and guide us give us glimpses of the Holy Spirit. This is because the Holy Spirit is a helper and guide. The Spirit, however, helps in ways that only God can. As Paul writes in his Letter to the Romans, "The love of God has been poured out into our hearts through the holy Spirit that has been given to us" (5:5). The Holy Spirit kindles the flame of faith in us. The Spirit enables us to know the Father and his Son, Jesus Christ. When sin separates us from God and the community, it is the Holy Spirit that makes forgiveness and new life possible.

In the Sacrament of Confirmation, before you are anointed, the bishop will say a special prayer for you and all the other candidates. He will ask the Father to send the Holy Spirit upon you to be your "Helper and Guide." Then he will ask that the seven Gifts of the Holy Spirit be given to you. In this chapter, we will

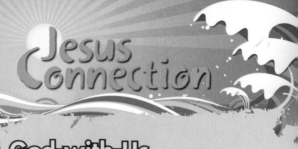

## Jesus Connection

### God-with-Us

Through the power of the Holy Spirit, Mary received the greatest gift in all of eternity. By the action of the Holy Spirit, Mary became the Mother of God. She gave birth to the Son of God, whose name is Emmanuel, which means "God-with-Us." Her son, Jesus, is truly the Son of God. Although he was born of a woman, he is the only Son of the Father; and he is God himself, the second Person of the Trinity. He is true God and true man. He took on our human nature, which means that the Son of God became one with us. We call this wonderful union of the human and divine natures in Jesus Christ the Incarnation.

The Father gave us this incredible gift of Jesus, his only Son. When we call Jesus the Son of God, we're describing a very unique relationship between the Father and the Son. There is only one Son of God who is also God himself: Jesus Christ.

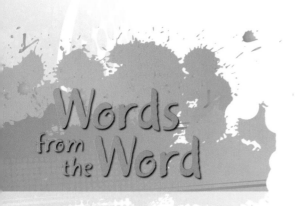

## Words from the Word

"The spirit of the LORD shall rest on him,
the spirit of wisdom and understanding,
the spirit of counsel and might,
the spirit of knowledge and the fear of the LORD."

(Isaiah 11:2–3, NRSV)

explore these gifts and their meaning. This will help you understand how the Spirit helps and guides us.

## The Gifts of the Holy Spirit

First, you may be wondering why there are *seven* Gifts of the Holy Spirit. In the Bible, the number seven is a symbolic number. Seven and multiples of seven (seventy, for example) mean perfection or completion or fullness. One example of this is that God finished the work of creating the world on the seventh day and rested (see Genesis 2:2). Another is when Jesus talks about forgiving others seventy-seven times (see Matthew 18:22).

The gifts of the Spirit are rooted in an Old Testament prophesy (see Isaiah 11:2–3; see also "Words from the Word" on this page). In this passage, Isaiah, writing many years before the birth of Jesus, is talking about the Messiah who is to come. The Spirit's gifts belong to Jesus Christ, the Messiah, fully and completely. When these gifts are given to us, they help us to live more fully and completely as followers of Jesus, sharing love with others.

In the Sacrament of Confirmation, the bishop prays that the following seven gifts will be given to all the candidates:

**Wisdom.** A wise person recognizes where the Holy Spirit is at work in the world.

**Understanding.** Understanding helps us to recognize how God wants us to live.

**Counsel.** This gift, also called right judgment, helps us to make choices that will lead us closer to God rather than away from God. The gift of counsel or right judgment helps us to figure out what God wants.

**Fortitude.** The gift of fortitude, also called courage, is the special help we need when faced with challenges or struggles.

**Knowledge.** This gift helps us to understand the meaning of what God has revealed, particularly the Good News of Jesus Christ.

**Piety.** This gift of piety, also called reverence, gives us a deep sense of respect for God and the Church. A reverent person honors God and approaches him with humility, trust, and love.

**Fear of the Lord.** The gift of fear of the Lord, also called wonder and awe, makes us aware of God's greatness and power.

Now let's explore what each of these gifts mean. Read each of the following scenarios and see if you can tell which Gifts of the Holy Spirit are being used.

## The Winter Dance

Molly was so excited! The dance was next Friday! Now that she and her friends were in seventh grade, they were finally old enough to go. Everyone was going to Amanda's house before the dance for pizza and pictures. Everyone was going, except for Taylor. Taylor wasn't invited. Molly, Amanda, and Taylor had been best friends since third grade. But Amanda was mad at Taylor.

Molly couldn't even remember why, but she knew Amanda had invited everyone but Taylor to her pre-dance party. Taylor said it was okay; she was just going to meet everyone at the dance. Molly couldn't let Taylor go by herself!

Molly was torn. She didn't want everyone to get mad at her for being on Taylor's side. And Molly and Amanda were still friends. She didn't want Amanda to get mad at *her* too. Besides, she wanted to go to Amanda's party. The pre-dance party would be more fun than the dance! But what about Taylor? What should Molly do?

Molly thought about it for days. She finally decided. She'd talk to Amanda, and if she couldn't convince her to invite Taylor, then she'd skip the party and just go to the dance with Taylor. Even if everyone got mad at *her* too. She had to do it for Taylor.

In this story, Molly had the _____

to face Amanda.

The Holy Spirit gave Molly the gift of _____.

## Awesome!

"Whoooaaa! That is so awesome!" Sam exclaimed. Powerful white waves were crashing over the jagged rocks. Sam had never seen the ocean before. He and his mom and brother had driven almost two days to get to the shore. While they were driving, he kept think-

We can see God's power and greatness in every part of life. Think about the great and wonderful things in your life. Name one of them.

ing: "What's the big deal? It's water." But, when he got there, it was a different story. It was magnificent. It was so beautiful that it was sort of mind-blowing! "God is pretty amazing to do this," Sam thought to himself.

Sam felt a sense of _____ when he saw the ocean.

The Holy Spirit gave him the gift of _____.

## The Bus Ride

Even though it was just a field trip to see a play, the bus ride was a blast! Everyone sat together and goofed around. The best seats were always in the back. As Staci waited on the steps to get up to the seats, she noticed Emily. Emily was sitting by herself in the second seat. Of course, everyone was passing by her. No one ever sat with Emily. It made Staci feel bad. "Love your neighbor as yourself." The words went through her head. She knew the words from the Bible. She knew what Jesus would do.

"Come on!" yelled Jordan from the back of the bus. "I saved you a seat!" "No, thanks," Staci replied. "I'm gonna sit here." And she sat down in the seat next to Emily.

Staci remembered the words of Jesus. She _____ what to do.

The Holy Spirit gave her the gift of _____.

# My Mission

### Using the Gifts

Choose one of the Gifts of the Holy Spirit that you wish you had more of. Do you wish you had more courage? wisdom? Then answer these questions:

Why would you like to see this gift more active in your life?

What will this gift enable you to do differently in your life?

## The Hundred-Year Flood

Robert was pretty depressed. His family had lost almost everything in the flood. They say a flood this bad hits only once every hundred years. And Robert's family didn't have flood insurance because they don't live in a so-called flood zone.

© Bill Alkofer/Corbis Sygma

God's gifts help us to see his presence and goodness, even in unlikely situations. Describe a time when you were able to see God's love in a bad situation.

With the help of neighbors, family, friends, classmates, and even strangers, Robert and his family cleaned up their house. As he helped his uncle rip up soggy carpet, Robert said: "It could've been worse. I think God was watching out for us. At least it wasn't a hurricane. That would've totally wiped us out. And no one got hurt. I didn't realize how many people really cared about us. I guess a bad thing can show you how much people care."

# Did You Know?

## The Fruits of the Spirit

There are seven Gifts of the Holy Spirit and twelve fruits of the Holy Spirit. You may be asking, "What's the difference between gifts and fruit?" Well, the "gifts" are the special graces we receive that help us to live the way God wants us to live. When we accept these gifts and live by the Spirit, good things become more and more present in our lives. We call these the "fruits of the Spirit." When we are filled with the Holy Spirit, we can be likened to plants or trees that bear great fruit. The twelve fruits of the Holy Spirit are love, joy, peace, patience, kindness, goodness, generosity, gentleness, faithfulness, modesty, self-control, and chastity. When you live by the Spirit, do you see these fruits springing up in your life?

Most of these fruits are probably very familiar to you. For example, you probably recognize love, joy, and peace in your life. But the last three fruits may not be as familiar to you as the others. Let's look at these three:

- **Modesty:** This means that you are appropriate, proper, and maybe a bit reserved in your dress, behavior, and speech. It means your actions reflect your God-given dignity. You are not overly flashy in the way you act and dress. You'll read about Mallory and her inappropriate shirt on the next page, noting that she changed into a shirt that was more modest.
- **Self-control:** This means you are in control of your temper, your actions, and your attitudes. You don't fly off the handle. You are not overly dramatic when it comes to expressing your emotions and feelings. You are in control of your body too. You care for your body and treat it with respect.
- **Chastity:** This means living your sexuality in a pure and healthy way. Jesus is a model of chastity. He calls us to be honest and healthy by respecting the sexuality of ourselves and others. A chaste person does not engage in sexual intercourse before marriage, but every person is called to be sexually pure, married or not.

**Dear God**

You shower us with many gifts.
The Gifts of the Holy
    Spirit are among the
    greatest of these gifts.
Help me to prepare for the
    outpouring of these
    gifts in the Sacrament
    of Confirmation.
Make me more aware of the
    ways I can use the gifts of
    wisdom, understanding,
    counsel, fortitude, knowledge,
    piety, and fear of the Lord
    in your presence.
I ask this in the name of your
    Son, Jesus, who lives and
    reigns with you and
    the Holy Spirit
    now and forever.
Amen.

Robert's comments are very _____ for a middle school-er. The Holy Spirit gave him the gift of _____.

## I Get It

"Okay, Mom, I get it," said Mallory, "I'll wear a different shirt." Mallory did get it. The shirt really wasn't appropriate for school. Mallory knew that. Although some girls would definitely have had a "tone" in their voice when they said, "I get it," Mallory didn't. She was actually pretty respectful when she answered her mom. She knew she shouldn't wear that shirt to school. She'd save it for another time.

Mallory _____ what her mom was saying.
The Holy Spirit had given her the gift of _____.

## Sunday-Night Youth Group

They weren't really supposed to use their cell phones in church, but it was just youth group. It wasn't Mass. They always ended Sunday-night youth group with a prayer service in the chapel. And besides, Mr. Wilson was nice. He wouldn't get mad if they were just texting.

But Tanaka felt uncomfortable having his phone out. He felt uncomfortable that the other guys were messing with their phones in chapel. "Come on, guys, quit it," he said quietly, just as Mr. Wilson started the prayer. And he moved up to the next row. It just wasn't right to mess around in church.

Tanaka showed _____ in the chapel.

The Holy Spirit gave him the gift of _____.

## The Sweatshirt

Courtney's mom was really mad that Courtney had lost her new sweatshirt. Her mom had just spent forty dollars on it and told Courtney that she'd have to pay back the money. Courtney had lost a couple of other sweatshirts too.

Later that same week, after track practice, Courtney found the *exact* same sweatshirt in the locker room. The only problem was that it was right in front of Jillian's locker. And Jillian had the same sweatshirt. But it *could* be Courtney's. If it *was* Jillian's, no one would ever know if Courtney just started wearing it. Then Courtney wouldn't have to pay her mom the forty dollars, and she'd be out of trouble. And besides, maybe it really was Courtney's. Jillian may have picked up Courtney's sweatshirt by mistake. Courtney could just say it was hers. No one was around. What should she do?

Does Courtney have the gift of _____? Will she make the right choice?

## Did You Get the Right Gift?

Let's see which gift you put with which story. Although one gift is matched with each story, there are some examples where more than one gift is at play in the story. This means that there is more than one "right" answer. That's how it works in life too. There may be many

Gifts of the Holy Spirit at work in our lives at the same time.

## The Gift of Fortitude

The story of Molly and the school dance was an example of the gift of fortitude. It took fortitude, or courage, for Molly to stand up to her best friend, Amanda. Molly took a risk. She did the courageous thing and stood up for her other best friend, Taylor.

## The Gift of Fear of the Lord

This was an easy one. Sam even said, "Awesome!" The gift of fear of the Lord means that we recognize God is awesome and does amazing things in our world!

## The Gift of Knowledge

Staci was quite knowledgeable of Jesus' teaching. Words from the Bible echoed in her head as she stood on the bus. Knowing the teachings of Jesus and the Church helped her to make the right choice. We don't just learn it all on our own. The Holy Spirit gives us the gift of knowledge.

## The Gift of Wisdom

Robert had received the gift of wisdom. He could look past the tragedy of the flood and see the good. He could see the Holy Spirit at work in others.

## The Gift of Understanding

Mallory understood what her mom was trying to say about her shirt. She understood that some clothing styles are just not appropriate at certain times. Mallory understood that some people

# Catholic Connection

## Gifts for the Church

The Gifts of the Holy Spirit are poured out on all the baptized members of the Church. The Holy Spirit is poured out on the Church herself. Jesus Christ is the head of the Church. The Church is the Body of Christ and the Temple of the Holy Spirit. The Holy Spirit gives life to the Church and makes her holy. The Spirit builds up the Church. The Spirit is the Church's source of life, helping her to fulfill her mission.

The Church's mission is the same as Christ's mission: to bring people into communion with God—Father, Son, and Holy Spirit. One of the ways the Church brings people into communion with God is through the Sacraments. And guess what? It's the Holy Spirit that enables us to see Christ's presence in the Sacraments. So, you see, the Holy Spirit is everywhere in the Church!

© Ariel Skelley/Blend Images/Corbis

The Gifts of the Holy Spirit are present in every member of the Church, helping the Church fulfill her mission. Which of the Spirit's gifts are at work in these young people?

get caught up in trying to be cool. She understands what it means to be a follower of Jesus.

### The Gift of Piety

The story about Tanaka in the chapel illustrates the gift of piety, or reverence. Tanaka was being respectful of God and Church even when the other kids weren't. The Holy Spirit helps us to be respectful of God, Church, and all of creation.

### The Gift of Counsel

Courtney had a tough decision to make with the sweatshirt. No one was watching, so she could do whatever she wanted without anyone seeing. The Holy Spirit guides us in those situations and helps us to make good choices. The Spirit gives us counsel, the ability to make the right judgment.

## Accepting the Gifts of the Holy Spirit

When the bishop extends his hands over you, he asks God to send the Holy Spirit. He prays that the Spirit's gifts will come upon you. It's not that the Holy Spirit wasn't with you before Confirmation; it's that now you'll have the Spirit with you in a deeper and fuller way. All you have to do is open your heart to the Spirit. It's a free gift—or rather seven free gifts!

Full of the Gifts of the Holy Spirit, you will be strengthened so you can more fully participate in the work of Jesus Christ. You will be bound more closely to the Church and to Christ. You will be a better, stronger, wiser, more courageous disciple. You will be strengthened to give even better witness to Christ by your words and actions. By accepting the Gifts of the Holy Spirit, you will help to increase the Spirit's power in the Church and in the world.

## Remembering a Gift

Remember a time when you received a great gift. Think of your favorite birthday gift or the best Christmas gift ever. Describe it below. Then look back at the Gifts of the Holy Spirit on page 71. Remember a time when you used one of these gifts. Was there a time when you showed understanding? courage? counsel? Describe how you used this gift. As you recall the gift you received and the gift you used, describe what makes each one important to you.

# 6 Being Anointed by the Holy Spirit

Have you ever . . . dipped your breadstick or pizza crust into oily garlic butter? applied antibiotic ointment to a cut or scrape? rubbed sunscreen all over your body to prevent sunburn? waited while your mom or dad pulled the car in for a 10-minute oil change? sautéed vegetables in olive oil? Are any of these experiences familiar to you? They give us just a glimpse into how often we use oil in daily life.

© Galina Barskaya/istockphoto.com

© HD Connelly/shutterstock.com

Life would be pretty dry and tasteless without oil. But what is the connection between oil and the Holy Spirit? You'll see!

Oil is basic to life. We use oils and butter in cooking to make food taste rich and delicious. Oil is used in medicine and ointments to help us heal. It is used in suntan lotion to protect our skin. Oil is used in cars, tractors, machinery, and bicycles to keep the parts lubricated and moving smoothly. Some oils are a type of dietary fat that is essential for the health of our brains. Professional athletes use oil to massage their sore muscles after a big game or a tough workout.

## Oil in Biblical Times

In biblical times, oil was very important to the people. It was a significant part of their diet, and because of its value, it was used in ceremonies and rituals. Leaders such as kings, prophets, and warriors were anointed with oil when they began their leadership roles. This was a sign that God was with them and would support them in their role. The Book of First Samuel, in the Old Testament, tells of David's being anointed king: "The LORD said to Samuel, 'This is the one—anoint him!' Samuel took the olive oil and anointed David in front

© Emin Ozkan/istockphoto.com

Once perfumes and spices are added to ordinary olive oil, it becomes a rich, aromatic symbol. How would it feel to have this oil poured on the top of your head?

The Bible tells how the prophet Samuel anointed David, King of Israel. Here, Samuel pours from a horn of oil while David's brothers watch. Look closely. Why do some of the brothers raise their hands?

of his brothers. Immediately the spirit of the LORD took control of David and was with him from that day on" (16:12–13, GNT).

In the Bible, oil is described as a necessity of life. It is a sign of God's goodness and love. The Book of Sirach, in the Old Testament, includes oil in its list of life's necessities, along with water, fire, iron, salt, flour, honey, milk, wine, and clothing (see 39:26). In the Book of Joel, also in the Old Testament, the Lord promises to send grain, wine, and oil to his people (see 2:19). This was a sign of his love and concern for his people. The Scriptures also tell of oil being used for healing wounds and soothing hurts. For example, the good Samaritan pours oil on the wounds of the man who has been beaten by robbers. The Bible also tells of oil being used for bathing and for relaxing athletes' muscles.

## Oil in the Sacraments

Jesus and many of his first followers were Jewish. During the early days of the Church, Christians drew upon this Jewish heritage. They adopted the practice of using oil to anoint new members

into the Christian community. Ever since, anointing with oil has been an important part of the Catholic Church's sacramental life.

Today the Church uses three different types of holy oils in liturgies:

- **Sacred Chrism** is olive oil with perfume that has been consecrated. It represents the sweet fragrance of Christ and the good works of his Body, the Church. Sacred Chrism is used in the Sacraments of Baptism, Confirmation, and Holy Orders and to consecrate objects, such as altars.

- **The Oil of Catechumens** is olive oil that has been blessed. It is used to anoint children and adults preparing for the Sacrament of Baptism. This helps the person resist evil. It's something like athletes who oiled their bodies before competitions in ancient times; the oil made it harder for competitors to grab and hold them.

- **The Oil of the Sick** is blessed olive oil used in the Sacrament of Anointing of the Sick. The priest anoints the forehead and hands of people who are seriously ill or near death. The anointing strengthens the sick and prepares those who are dying for death.

In this chapter, we will focus on Sacred Chrism and the meaning of being anointed with it in Confirmation.

## Jesus Connection

## Jesus the Christ

Did you realize that Christ isn't Jesus' last name? The word *Christ* is a title the early Christians gave to Jesus. The word *Christ* means "anointed one" or "messiah." Jesus' followers came to realize that Jesus wasn't an ordinary religious leader. They came to see he was the chosen one of God, or the "anointed one." The biblical accounts of Jesus' Baptism tell of his being anointed by the Holy Spirit. The disciples recognized Jesus as the one who would save them from sin and lead them to everlasting life. Peter is one of the first disciples to recognize Jesus. In Mark 8:29, Peter says, "You are the Messiah." Jesus' name and title have been fused into one. Jesus is the Christ, the Messiah, the anointed one.

## Sacred Chrism: Not Just Any Oil

Sacred Chrism is consecrated by a bishop. To consecrate something is to make it holy. The bishop asks God the Father to fill the mixture of oil and perfume with the power of the Holy Spirit through Christ. He prays that everyone who will be anointed will radiate the goodness of life and live forever with God. This includes you and all your peers who will be anointed at Confirmation.

Without looking at the previous page, can you name these three holy oils of the Church? Can you name which oil is used in which Sacrament? Look at the picture for clues.

sick

chrism

catechumens

© Zulhazmi Zabri/shutterstock.com

The bishop usually consecrates Sacred Chrism once a year during a special Mass on Holy Thursday, the Thursday just before Easter Sunday (see "Blessing of Chrism" in appendix A for one of the bishop's prayer options for the consecration). Then he shares this holy oil with all the parishes of his diocese. If you've never seen your parish's Sacred Chrism or other blessed oils, look around next time you go to Mass. The oils are usually displayed in fancy bottles in a special glass case so people can see them.

Now, let's take a closer look at what it means to be anointed in the Sacrament of Confirmation.

## More Like Christ

Your friendship with Jesus Christ is kind of like your relationship with a friend. Deepening your relationship with Christ is like deepening your relationship with a friend. Think about it this way. Say you and one of your neighbors or classmates have been friends since preschool. You've had lots of good times and some bad times. As the years go by, you get to know each other better and better. You support and help each other. You become even closer friends. The bond of friendship grows.

In Confirmation the bond between you and Jesus Christ grows deeper. When you were baptized, you were united to Jesus Christ and the Church. As mentioned earlier, you were even anointed with Sacred Chrism. This was a sign that you were given the gift of the Holy Spirit. You gained a new identity and a new name: Christian. (The word *Christian* comes from the Greek word *christos*, which means "anointed one.") When you celebrate the Sacrament of Confirmation, you will be anointed with Sacred Chrism again. The bishop will lay hands on you and anoint you on the forehead. Along with this gesture, he will say your name followed by the words "Be sealed with the Gift of the Holy Spirit" (*Order of Confirmation*, number 27). This anointing will confirm the anointing you received at your Baptism. Through the Gifts of the Holy Spirit, you will become more like Christ. Your relationship with Christ and your connection to the Church will become stronger.

Another way to think about how the Holy Spirit makes us like Christ is to think about being formed or molded. Imagine for a

Help me to be more like your
    Son, Jesus Christ.
    Even though I try,
    sometimes it's hard.
Help me to be kind and
    fair and loving like he was.
Fill me with the power of
    the Holy Spirit. Help me
    to open my heart to your
    never-ending love.
Amen.

# Words from the Word

> "The one who . . . anointed us is God; he has also put his seal upon us and given the Spirit in our hearts." (2 Corinthians 1:21–22)

moment that you have a piece of clay in your hands. Work with it and give it a form. Now imagine that you are the clay and the Holy Spirit is the potter. Imagine the Holy Spirit's shaping and molding everything that makes you who you are—mind, body, heart, and soul. Your anointing in Confirmation will be a celebration of the Holy Spirit at work in your life. Every day the Spirit is with you, shaping and molding you to be the best you that you can possibly be. The Holy Spirit is molding you so that you are more fully an image of Christ. Through Confirmation you are made to be like Christ more than ever before in your life.

Just what do you look like if you're made in the image of Christ? Well, for one thing, you try to be kind to everyone. You treat other kids and adults with respect. Jesus cared about the feelings of other people.

The Grand Canyon was shaped by the power of water and wind. God forms you by the power of the Holy Spirit.

© Christophe Testi/shutterstock.com

Another way you can be like Christ is to help others. Jesus fed people who were hungry, cured people who were sick, and forgave those who had sinned. You can help people in many ways. For example, you might invite a classmate who is often alone to sit with you and your friends at lunch. You might say a comforting word to a student in your class whose family has experienced a loss. You might stop someone from spreading a bad rumor. You can remember other people in need in your prayers. You might also take the time to visit with and pray with an elderly neighbor or relative. You could also volunteer to help with vacation Bible school or a religious education program for young children. If you have younger siblings, you might help them learn about stories from the Bible. You might forgive a friend who has hurt your feelings. These are just some of the ways you can be like Christ.

## Sacred Chrism Marks Us—Permanently!

When is the last time you got permanent (also called indelible) marker on your skin? It left a mark, but it eventually came off, didn't it? Well, the mark left by the Sacred Chrism is a little different. It's a mark on your soul, and it really is *permanent*. It can never be removed. Another term for a mark is "character," so you may hear this permanent mark referred to as an 'indelible character.' The mark left on your soul is the mark of the Holy Spirit. It

## Right from the Rite

""By this gift of the Holy Spirit the faithful are more fully conformed to Christ and are strengthened with the power to bear witness to Christ for the building up of his Body in faith and charity. They are marked with the character or seal of the Lord in such a way that the Sacrament of Confirmation cannot be repeated." (*Order of Confirmation*, number 2)

means that the Holy Spirit will always be with you and in you to guide and strengthen you.

The Church also calls this mark of the Holy Spirit, the *seal* of the Holy Spirit. A seal is a sign of ownership. A brand is a type of seal. When a rancher brands horses or cattle, the brand shows who owns the animal. The seal of a city is a sign or a symbol of that city. All the trucks, cars, snowplows, and parks owned by the city carry the city seal. Sometimes official documents are sealed with a raised symbol or sign to show they are official. Dig out your birth certificate or your baptismal certificate and see if it has been sealed.

In the Sacrament of Confirmation, you are sealed with the gift of the Holy Spirit. The seal says you are officially a fully initiated Christian. The seal of the Holy Spirit shows that you belong to Christ. The Sacred Chrism is rubbed all over your forehead as a sign of the sealing. Because the seal lasts forever, the Sacrament of Confirmation is never repeated. You are confirmed only once in your life.

## The Bishop

Just who does this anointing with Sacred Chrism in Confirmation? As we discussed in chapter 4, it was the bishop who was the original minister of

A seal shows that a diploma, license, or other document is official. The seal of the Holy Spirit is the sacred, permanent mark of Confirmation.

© Stefan Klein/istockphoto.com

Confirmation. This continues to be the practice in most dioceses in the United States. When the bishop is the minister for Confirmation, his actions remind us of the first Apostles. This is because he is a successor of the first Apostles. Do you recall the story of Pentecost when the Holy Spirit came upon the Apostles? After that they went out and gave the Holy Spirit to others by the laying on of hands.

Bishops are successors of the Apostles because we can trace each and every bishop back to the original Apostles. It works like this: Your bishop was ordained by a bishop who was ordained by a bishop before him. And that bishop was ordained by a bishop who was ordained by the bishop before him. Get the idea? If you keep going, you can get all the way back to the Twelve Apostles. So when the bishop anoints you, it is a reminder that you are connected to the whole Church and that you share in the work of the Church.

## Confirmation Binds Us to the Church

The Church is the Body of Christ. So when we are united to Christ, we are also united to the Church. The bonds with our Church grow stronger through Confirmation. With this closer bond comes some responsibility. Once confirmed you become a fuller member of the Catholic Church. You are expected to be more actively involved in the work of the Church. In other words, you have a bigger part to play in the mission of the Church.

The mission of the Church is to spread the Good News and continue

# Catholic Connection

## The Church

When you hear the word *church*, do you tend to think of the building you go to for Sunday Mass? It is so much more than a building!

The Church is a community, but not exactly like groups we might decide to join. *Church* means "convocation," which is related to the verb *convoke*. To convoke is to call people together. The Church is the community of people who have been called together by God. This isn't an exclusive club, however. God calls everyone.

It is important to understand that the Church is more than what the eye can see. She is one but is made up of two components, human and divine. We see the visible reality of the Church in such things as people gathered for the Eucharist; the church buildings; the Pope, bishops, and priests; young people praying on retreats and serving others; the Bible; and so on. But the Church is more than what we can see. The Church is also a spiritual reality. This is a mystery that we see only with the eyes of faith. It builds on the visible reality. Through the action of the Holy Spirit, the aspects of the Church that we can see communicate and put us in touch with the divine component of the Church. Because the Church helps us to "see" divine realities, the Church is sometimes referred to as a sacrament. This is because sacraments are encounters with Jesus Christ that help us to see that God is with us. The Church makes visible the communion we share with God—Father, Son, and Holy Spirit.

The Holy Spirit assures us that the Church is carrying out Christ's mission, despite the sins and failures of the members. Through us God is doing what we could never do on our own. Our work is a participation in the real, but unseen, divine life of the Trinity. Through Confirmation and the action of the Holy Spirit, our participation deepens.

the work of Jesus Christ. This means that as a disciple of Jesus Christ, you are called to think about how you can cooperate with the Holy Spirit and continue the work of Jesus. How can you help others hear the Gospel message through your words and actions?

Jesus came to call everyone to gather into God's family and to share in divine life. He reached out especially to those who were poor and sick and those who were sinners and outcasts. Jesus sent his disciples to continue his work by making others his disciples. Jesus said, "Go, therefore, and make disciples of all nations, baptizing them in the name of the Father, and of the Son, and of the holy Spirit" (Matthew 28:19).

You may not be traveling to other nations anytime soon. And you may never have occasion to baptize someone. But you are definitely able to do plenty of things that help to continue Jesus' work.

All in all, it's an honor and a responsibility to be confirmed. Through the Holy Spirit, you will become more like Christ. You will become more fully the person God made you to be. It is a responsibility to live up to the name you were first marked with at Baptism: "Christian" or "anointed one."

# My Mission

## The Church's Mission

Once you are anointed with Sacred Chrism in Confirmation, you have a bigger role to play in the mission of the Church. What are some ways you can continue the mission of Jesus Christ? Be specific. Be concrete. Name three things you can do.

1.



2.



3.

## Images of the Church

Three New Testament images reflect a powerful connection between the Church and the Trinity. The images help us to see that the universal Church is a people brought into unity from the unity of the three Persons.

### People of God

Long ago God chose the Israelites to be his people. He established an everlasting covenant, or special relationship, built on mutual promises with them through Noah, Abraham, and Moses. Through Moses he revealed his law, the Ten Commandments. Then through Jesus Christ, God fully revealed himself and established his Covenant forever. He did this to fulfill his desire to make all people one body united in love through the Holy Spirit. Those who believe in Christ are the new people of God, "God's people" (1 Peter 2:10). All are called to enter this one family, the Church, through faith and Baptism.

### Body of Christ

Christ establishes the community of believers as his own Body. Saint Paul explains: "Christ is like a single body, which has many parts. . . . All of you are Christ's body" (1 Corinthians 12:12,27, GNT). Comparing the Church with the body shows her bond with Christ. All members, though diverse, are united with one another and with Christ, the head of the body. The union of the members with Jesus is also expressed by referring to the Church as the Bride of Christ. Christ, the bridegroom, loved the Church, the bride, so much that he formed an everlasting covenant with her.

### Temple of the Holy Spirit

The Church is the dwelling place of the Holy Spirit. Saint Paul said to the people of Corinth, "Do you not know that you are the temple of God, and that the spirit of God dwells in you?" (1 Corinthians 3:16). Jesus Christ has poured out the Spirit on the members of the Church, making the Holy Spirit part of everything the Church is and does. The Spirit gives the Church unity, even though her members are all different. The Holy Spirit gives life to the Church and is the source of all her gifts.

## Being More Like Christ

Why do you want to be more like Jesus Christ? Would it make your life harder or easier?
Think about it and write your response in this space.

Why do you want to be a "fuller member" of the Catholic Church? Would it mean more
work for you or less? Think about it and write your response in this space.

# 7 The Eucharist: The Heart of the Church's Life

Lunch hour is the best part of the day for Logan. All the eighth graders eat together during sixth period. There is a mass exodus as everyone leaves the second floor and walks down to the cafeteria. Groups of twos, threes, and fours, as well as singles, walk together, some with lunch sacks in their hands. Logan walks with Mark, Travis, and Carly. They always sit at the same table off to the left by the windows. It's a long table, and it quickly fills with kids, lunch trays, milk cartons, Gatorade bottles, snack bags, backpacks, and jackets.

Eating meals with friends and family is an important, life-giving event. What good memories do you have of eating a special meal with others?

© Ariel Skelley/Blend Images/Corbis

Principal Myers calls lunch hour "middle school madness." But to Logan it's wonderful! It's the one time during the day she can be with friends, find out what's going on with everyone, eat, drink, and just hang out. It's a time to be together and also to take a break. Plus, it helps her to refuel so she can get through those last afternoon classes!

At the end of lunch, Principal Myers dismisses everyone back to class. Logan files out with Mark, Travis, and Carly, plus a couple other kids. Everybody heads out for an afternoon of classes, walking, talking, laughing, and ready to face another three hours of life in middle school.

## Special Meals and Mass

If going to the school cafeteria is not exactly the high point of your day, then think of another time when you really enjoy gathering around a table with friends and family. Maybe it's dinner on Thanksgiving, Christmas, or Easter Sunday, or a memorable birthday or anniversary celebration.

Special meals with friends or family have some things in common with the Mass. The basic parts often follow a similar pattern. Look at Logan's lunch with her friends. She got together with her friends and they walked to the cafeteria together. At the beginning of Mass, we gather together and participate in the Introductory Rites. At lunchtime Logan and her friends talk, listen, and tell one another what is going on in their day. At Mass we listen to the Word of God and hear how God is working in our lives. At lunch everyone takes their food out of their lunch bags or goes through the cafeteria line and brings their food to the table. At Mass

## Jesus Is Here

Jesus is always with us. But in the Eucharist, Jesus Christ is present in a special way. This is why we say that the Eucharist is the heart of the Church's life. Jesus Christ is present at the Mass in several ways:

+ in the community gathered
+ in the Word of God
+ in the priest or bishop who is presiding
+ in the Eucharistic species

Christ is most especially present in the Eucharistic species, which refers to the bread and wine after they have been converted into Christ's Body and Blood. During the Eucharistic Prayer when the celebrant prays over the bread and wine and repeats Jesus' words from the Last Supper, the bread and wine become the Body and Blood of Jesus Christ. This change is called Transubstantiation. The bread and wine become Christ himself. He becomes present in a true, real, and concrete way. He is fully present in Body, Blood, soul, and divinity.

we bring the bread and wine to the altar. Most kids don't say grace out loud before eating lunch at school, but some offer thanks to God silently. If you were at home, you'd probably say grace before you ate, especially at dinner or at special meals. At Mass the priest prays a prayer of thanksgiving called the Eucharistic Prayer. Then we receive our food, the Body and Blood of Christ. At the end of lunch, Principal Myers dismisses the eighth graders from the cafeteria. At the end of special meals at home, people wish one another well and say good-bye. At Mass, having received the food of eternal life, the priest dismisses us to love and serve the Lord. Paying attention to the pattern of your special meals with family and friends may help you to recognize the pattern of our Eucharist celebrations.

## The High Point of Catholic Life

Participating in the Mass on Sundays (or the vigil on Saturday evenings) is the most important thing we do. The Eucharistic table is where we gather with the Christian community to "refuel" our souls for the upcoming week. We come to the altar with our Christian family to be nourished by Christ's Body and Blood. We come to the table of the Lord to eat the food of eternal life. Celebrating the Eucharist is the high point of Catholic life. This is why Confirmation is usually celebrated within the Mass.

Mass always includes the following:

- the proclamation of the Word of God
- prayers of thanksgiving to God the Father for all he does for us, especially giving us the gift of his Son, Jesus Christ
- the consecration of the bread and wine
- the reception of the Body and Blood of Christ during Communion

All of these elements that make up the Mass form one single act of worship. On the day of your Confirmation, the laying on of hands and the anointing with Sacred Chrism will also be a part of this act of worship.

Here, it's important to notice a few things about Confirmation's being celebrated within the Mass. First, we hear

© Bill Wittman

the Word of God as part of the celebration of Confirmation. This is significant because the Holy Spirit flows to us from the hearing of the Word. And we come to know God's will for us when we hear the Word.

Second, celebrating Confirmation within the Mass helps to make clear that Confirmation is strongly connected

Listening to the Word of God during Mass draws us closer to God. How will you open your heart for the proclamation of God's Word during the celebration of the Sacrament of Confirmation?

# Catholic Connection

## The Eucharist Is a Sacrifice

When was the last time you made a sacrifice? Did you sacrifice doing something fun in order to help with the dishes? Hopefully, you know what it's like to make little sacrifices. Our best sacrifices are made out of love. A true sacrifice is a giving of oneself.

It is hard to imagine making the sacrifice Jesus made. Jesus gave his whole self for all people of all time because he loved us so much. He died for our sins in order to free us from the slavery of sin. We call this reparation because Jesus repaired, or made amends for, our sins. Because Jesus wiped away our sins, we can have eternal life with God in Heaven.

The Eucharist is a sacrifice. In the Eucharist, we call to mind Jesus' sacrifice. But we do more than just remember. Because we are members of the Body of Christ we are joined to Christ's sacrifice. It's not that Jesus is sacrificing again at each Mass. Christ gave his fullest, best self in thanksgiving to the Father when he offered himself on the Cross, once for all. Through Christ's one perfect offering, which is re-presented in the liturgy, we receive the grace of that perfect love between the Father and Son in the Holy Spirit.

© Brooklyn Museum/Corbis

In the Eucharist we recall how Jesus made the ultimate sacrifice out of love for us. Think about the "little" sacrifices you make...Name some of the people for whom you make those sacrifices.

to the Eucharist and the whole of Christian initiation. As mentioned in chapter 1, Baptism, Confirmation, and the Eucharist are the Sacraments of Christian Initiation. We'll talk more about these three Sacraments a little later in the chapter (see "Initiation and the Paschal Mystery," pages 104–105).

Third, celebrating Confirmation within the Mass reminds us that the Holy Spirit works to bring us into communion with one another and with Christ so that we become more and more the Body of Christ. Confirmation, as well as all the other Sacraments and the whole of life, are oriented to the Eucharist. The bishop doesn't just send you home after you've been confirmed. He invites you to celebrate the Liturgy of the Eucharist and to receive the Body and Blood of Christ, which nourish you so that you might continue Jesus' mission in your daily life.

© Bill Wittman

What parts of Jesus' mission are hardest for you? Forgiving others? Loving your enemies, or yourself? Something else? The Eucharist can strengthen you!

# My Mission

## To Love and to Serve

In Confirmation you receive the Holy Spirit, which completes your initiation and strengthens you to carry out the mission of Jesus Christ and the Church. But remember that every Mass ends by sending us forth in mission. The priest says this or something similar to it: "Go and announce the Gospel of the Lord" (*Roman Missal*). Name two specific things you will do this week to announce the Gospel through your love and service of others.

**1.**


**2.**

## From Sacrament to Mission

Confirmation fills us with the Holy Spirit and leads us to the Eucharist, which nourishes us with the spiritual food we need to carry out the Church's mission in the world. Confirmation and the Eucharist, as well as all the other Sacraments, propel us outward, focusing our attention on the needs of others more than on our own needs. Through the action of the Holy Spirit, Confirmation deepens the grace we receive in Baptism. It unites us more firmly to Christ. It makes us more like Christ and gives us the strength and gifts we need to truly be Jesus' disciples. We witness to Christ when we continue his mission and strive to do what he would do.

The nourishment we receive in the Eucharist is very important in our lives. We eat and drink the Body and Blood of Christ so we can go forth to continue the work of Christ. The priest dismisses us at the end of the Mass using these or similar words: "Go forth to love and to serve the Lord." That's exactly what we must do. We must serve the Lord by continuing his mission. His mission, which is now the Church's mission too, is to proclaim the Reign of God and bring others into union with God.

How do we proclaim the Reign of God and bring others closer to God? We try to act as Jesus would act. We try to do what Jesus would do: help people who are poor, be kind to our enemies, tell others about the Good News through our words and actions, participate in the life of the Christian community, be good stewards of creation, welcome new kids at school, feed those who are hungry, pray, forgive people who might be mean to us, respect the life and God-given dignity

Each of us has a role in the mission of the Church. Once you have received the Holy Spirit in the Sacrament of Confirmation, what will your new role be?

of all people, be compassionate, love everyone . . . yes, *everyone.*

Continuing the mission of Jesus Christ is a big job. Rest assured that we are not left on our own to do this. The Holy Spirit helps us to continue the mission of Jesus, empowering and strengthening us for our mission.

## Right from the Rite

"As a rule, Confirmation takes place within Mass so that the fundamental connection of this Sacrament with all of Christian Initiation, which reaches its culmination in the Communion of the Body and Blood of Christ, may stand out in a clearer light." (*Order of Confirmation*, number 13)

You give us your Son,
    Jesus, in the Eucharist.
Help me to receive the Body
    and Blood of Christ with
    an open and loving heart.
I ask that your Holy Spirit
    will help me go forth
    from every Mass
    proclaiming your
    goodness with my
    actions and my attitude.
May the Holy Spirit help me
    to become more like your
    Son, Jesus, who lives and
    reigns forever and
    ever.
Amen.

## Initiation and the Paschal Mystery

Baptism, Confirmation, and the Eucharist form a unity. Together they lay the foundation for our lives as Christians. That's why these three are called the Sacraments of Christian Initiation. From the very first moment of our Baptism, we are united with God. God wants to share his life with us. Thus, we share in the divine life. One important thing this means is that we participate in a special mystery that is central to Christianity. This mystery is called the Paschal Mystery. It is the mystery of how Jesus' suffering, death, Resurrection, and Ascension into Heaven save us from sin and death. His death frees us from sin, and his Resurrection makes new life possible. Let's look at how the three Sacraments of Initiation lay the foundation of our Christian life and incorporate us into the mystery of Christ's dying and rising.

### Baptism

Baptism frees us from sin and gives us new life with God. It makes us one with Christ. When we are united to Christ in Baptism, we are also united to the Paschal Mystery. When we go down into the waters of Baptism (or have the water poured on our heads), our sins are washed away and we rise from the waters as a new creation. We become children of God, sisters or brothers of Christ. We are united to Christ's death and Resurrection. Our sins die, and we receive new life in Christ. We are bonded to Christ and to his great passing over from death to new life (see the "Did you Know?" sidebar on page 106 for more on Passover).

If you've ever participated in the Easter Vigil, celebrated on the Saturday night before Easter, you've heard these verses from Paul's letter to the Romans proclaimed: "Are you unaware that we who were baptized into Christ Jesus were baptized into his death? . . . If, then, we have died with Christ, we believe that we shall also live with him" (6:3,8).

## Confirmation

Confirmation seals Baptism and binds us more tightly to the Church and to Christ. It involves completing or perfecting what happens in Baptism. We are united with Christ in Baptism, and now in Confirmation we become more like Christ. We are also more closely bound to the Paschal Mystery, more deeply connected to Jesus' death and Resurrection and the promise of eternal life.

## The Eucharist

We share in Christ's Body and Blood in the Eucharist. All Seven Sacraments celebrate the Paschal Mystery, but the Eucharist is the ultimate celebration of the Paschal Mystery. This is because Christ himself is in the Eucharist in a special way. We actually participate in the Paschal Sacrifice (see the "Did you Know?" sidebar

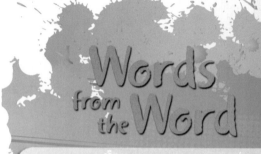

**Words from the Word**

"While they were eating, he took bread, said the blessing, broke it, and gave it to them, and said, 'Take it; this is my body.' Then he took a cup, gave thanks, and gave it to them, and they all drank from it. He said to them, 'This is my blood of the covenant, which will be shed for many.'" (Mark 14:22–24)

### Paschal Means "Passover"

You've probably heard the word *paschal* many times: Paschal Lamb, Paschal Mystery, Paschal candle. *Paschal* comes from a Greek word that means "Passover." Christians' use of the word *paschal* is rooted in the very first Passover.

The first Passover refers to that great event when the Israelites "passed over" from a life of slavery in Egypt to freedom. In the Book of Exodus, we hear how God sent the angel of death to kill all the firstborn in the land of Egypt. The Israelites' firstborn were spared, however. The Lord instructed Moses to tell the Israelites to kill young lambs and put the blood of the lambs on their doorposts. This was the sign for the angel of death to "pass over" the homes of the Israelites. The Israelites then roasted the lambs and ate them with unleavened bread. Leaven makes bread rise and takes time. The Israelites ate their bread without leaven because they were in a hurry, preparing for their journey out of Egypt.

This was the first Passover meal. Throughout history, and still today, Jewish people celebrate Passover.

The New Testament refers to Jesus as the Lamb of God (see John 1:29) and the Paschal Lamb (see 1 Corinthians 5:7). Like the Israelites' lamb, Jesus was sacrificed so others would be free. Jesus' blood was poured out to save us from sin and death. That's not the end of the story though. Jesus was raised from the dead. By the power of the Holy Spirit, Jesus "passed over" from death to new life.

The Church's Sacraments and liturgies celebrate the Paschal Mystery or Christ's Passover. Especially in the Eucharist, we celebrate Jesus Christ's "passing over" from his death on the cross to new life with the Father. The saving events of Christ's Passover are actually made present in the Eucharist, and we participate in them. Through the working of the Holy Spirit, we share in Christ's new life!

on page 106 for more on Paschal and the "Catholic Connection" sidebar on page 100 for more on sacrifice). During the Mass, we participate in Christ's dying and rising.

## Participating in the Paschal Mystery

The great news at the heart of the Paschal Mystery is that Christ is risen and lives in our hearts. Christ and his Resurrection are the source of our belief that death is not the end for us and that one day after death we too will be resurrected. That is the ultimate way we will participate in the Paschal Mystery.

In the meantime, the events of our daily lives give us glimpses into the mystery of passing from death to new life. Think of death in a figurative rather than literal way. For example, the loss of a friendship can be like a death. Let's say a friend of yours starts a horrible rumor about you. You are deeply hurt by this ugly rumor. Your friendship is destroyed. This is like a death. Then imagine your friend's being very sorry and apologizing to you. Your friendship is restored and becomes life-giving. This shows the pattern of the Paschal Mystery. Your friendship had "died" because of sin. You may have even felt like you had "died" in a way. Even though it may have been hard, you believed in the power of forgiveness; thus, you and your friendship were restored to "new life."

There are many other examples of what we might call "little" everyday dyings and risings. You fail a test but work hard and get a B on the next one. Your mom loses her job. Eventually, she finds a new job, which is even better than the first. You are devastated when you have to move to a new school or a new town. Eventually, you make new friends and love your new place! Your mom and dad get divorced, and your old way of being a family ends. But you find a new way of life and a new way of being family.

These are just a few of examples that give us a sense of the Paschal Mystery of Christ's dying and rising. We celebrate Christ's dying and rising whenever we participate in the Sacraments. And we live with hope because of the promise of resurrection after death. In the meantime, knowing that the risen Christ is present in our hearts brings us great joy.

## The Promise of Resurrection after Death

Because of Christ's dying and rising, we live with great hope. We know that death will not be the end for us and that we will rise on the last day. At death,

© Brooklyn Museum/Corbis

The Apostles experienced the Risen Christ in a unique and special way. In the Paschal Mystery, we participate in Christ's Death and Resurrection. When have you experienced "death and new life"?

our souls are separated from our bodies, but in the resurrection, God will make our bodies rise again and be transformed. God wants us to be with him in Heaven forever. He doesn't force us, however, to live the kind of life that leads to eternal happiness with him. We choose how to live and that determines what happens after death. If we turn away from God, refuse to love and think only of ourselves, we risk the reality of Hell, or eternal separation from God.

At the time of our death, Christ will judge us. He will compare how we have lived with the message of the Gospel. This is called the particular judgment. Paul summed it up this way: "For all of us must appear before Christ, to be judged by him. We will each receive what we deserve, according to everything we have done, good or bad, in our bodily life" (2 Corinthians 5:10, GNT).

# Back to the Eucharist

Every week when you come back to the Eucharist, remember that we celebrate the Paschal Mystery. We come back to celebrate the mystery that death is not what it seems. Death opens the way to new and eternal life with God.

Your Confirmation is part of the Church's celebration of the Paschal Mystery. The day you are confirmed, remember that you are becoming a fully initiated member of the Catholic Church. Initiation is a beginning, not a graduation. After Confirmation you will receive the Body and Blood of Christ, and then you will be sent forth. Each week you will be called back to the Eucharist to celebrate what Christ has done for us. Our participation in the Sunday Mass (or the vigil on Saturday evening) is so important for our own lives and the life of the Church that we are obligated to attend. The Eucharist nourishes us and strengthens us to carry out the mission of the Church.

## At the Table

Picture your favorite table. Is it your kitchen table? your grandparents' dining room table? the corner table at McDonald's? How is Jesus present at this table?

# 8 Celebrating the Sacrament of Confirmation

When was the last time you were really excited for a big celebration? Was it the end-of-the-year field trip or party at school? Was it your family's Christmas celebration? Was it your birthday? or maybe a friend's birthday party? What made this event important to you?

© Zave Smith/Corbis

A party is a celebration of life. Sacraments are celebrations of God's life in us and ours in God. How will you prepare to celebrate Confirmation?

When it's almost time for a party, a celebration, or some other big event, you probably spend time thinking about it. Remember back to a special celebration from the past. What thoughts were going through your mind ahead of time? Maybe something like: "I can't wait! This is going to be so cool! I've been waiting for so long! I wonder what it will be like. I'm so ready for this!"

What feelings did you have as you waited for the big event? Were you nervous, excited, unsure, happy, confident, raring to go, indifferent? Did you talk to your family and friends about how you were feeling? Were others around you awaiting the same event?

What did you do to get ready for the big event? If it was your party, did you send out invitations? If it was a big field trip, did you have to have a permission slip signed? Did you have to pack a backpack or do an assignment before the trip? If it was a Christmas celebration, what did you do to get ready for it?

Well, it's time for final preparations for a big event—the celebration of the Sacrament of Confirmation. It's almost here!

# Final Preparation for the Sacrament of Confirmation

You've spent months getting ready to celebrate the Sacrament of Confirmation. Let's review some of what you've done. Then we'll look ahead to what still needs to be done before you are confirmed.

## What You've Done to Prepare

Over the past weeks or months, you've done a lot of different things to get ready for the Sacrament of Confirmation. You've probably done most or all of the following:

- accepted the role and responsibilities of being a candidate
- chosen a sponsor

- decided on your Confirmation name
- reflected on the meaning of your Baptism
- learned about the outpouring of the Holy Spirit
- thought carefully about the Gifts of the Holy Spirit
- learned about the meaning and importance of being anointed with Sacred Chrism in Confirmation and becoming more like Christ
- studied the connection between Baptism, Confirmation, and the Eucharist
- reviewed some of the Church's central doctrines, such as the Trinity and the Paschal Mystery
- reflected on how you carry out the mission of Jesus and how you will do so more fully after Confirmation

You've taken seriously your responsibility to prepare for Confirmation. That shows you're serious about being a disciple of Jesus Christ and about being a full member of the Catholic Church. Now you're ready for the final steps of your Confirmation preparation process.

# Jesus Connection

## Like God's Own Son

Have you ever wanted to be like someone else? Well, that can be a good thing or a bad thing. In Confirmation it's a good thing. In Confirmation you become more like Christ.

By the power of the Holy Spirit, we become more and more the people God wants us to be. In Baptism we become adopted daughters and sons of God. In Confirmation, which completes our Baptism, our bonds with the Father's only Son, Jesus Christ, and with the Church grow stronger through the action of the Holy Spirit. We are empowered to become more like Christ. In fact, Jesus is a divine Person who took on our human nature and became one of us so that we might become divine. Through the power of the Holy Spirit, we come to share in the divine nature.

## What You Still Need to Do to Prepare

### Pray

Pray to God about receiving the Sacrament of Confirmation. Take some time at night before you go to bed to pray, or, while you're in the car or listening to music, turn down the volume and pray about this upcoming celebration. The *Catechism of the Catholic Church* describes prayer as "the raising of one's mind and heart to God or the requesting of good things from God" (St. John Damascene, *De fide orth.* 3, 24: PG 94, 1089C) (number 2590).

If you're not sure how to begin, here are some things to think about:

- Tell God your thoughts about receiving the Sacrament.
- Talk about why being confirmed is important to you.
- Ask God to bless you and all who will be confirmed with you.

- Talk about your heart. Is there anything about your heart that needs to soften or change before you are confirmed?
- Be silent and listen.
- Offer thanks for the many good things God has done.
- Pray the Lord's Prayer (see appendix A). The Church calls this the quintessential prayer because it is a perfect example of conversation with God and a perfect way for us to pray.
- Pray for all those in need and ask for the help you need to serve others.
- Pray in thanksgiving for all those who have helped you to grow in faith during your childhood.
- Review the Ten Commandments (see appendix B) and the Beatitudes (see Matthew 5:1–12 or appendix B) and reflect on how you are living your life. Pray to God for the guidance and strength to make any needed changes.

Jesus taught the disciples how to pray. You are one of the disciples. What can you learn from Jesus about prayer? How did he pray? Check out Matthew 6:5–13.

In addition to daily prayers on your own, the Church invites you to participate regularly in liturgy. This includes attending Mass on Sundays and feast days as well as praying the Liturgy of the Hours, a special cycle of prayers for times of the day, especially morning and evening.

### Talk to Your Sponsor

If you haven't spoken with your sponsor recently, get in touch with him or her in a personal way. Try to get together, but if that's not possible, at least try to talk on the phone. If you're not sure what to say, here are some talking points:

- Start by thanking her or him (again!) for being your sponsor.
- Make sure your sponsor knows the time and place for the rehearsal and for the celebration of Confirmation.
- Ask if she or he has any questions

© Bill Wittman

Your sponsor is eager to talk, listen, and share. Take advantage of this special relationship and turn to your sponsor for friendship, help, and support. What would you like to say to your sponsor?

about the celebration.

- If you are not using your baptismal name, remind your sponsor about the name you've chosen. She or he will tell it to the bishop right before you are anointed.
- Tell your sponsor you are glad that she or he is your sponsor. Give specific reasons.

### Bring to Mind Your Confirmation Name

By now you've decided to choose the name of a saint—someone whose

# Did You Know?

## Keys to Happiness

What is the source of happiness? Money? fame? a report card full of A's? gold medals earned in competition? nice clothes? lots of friends? the latest technological devices? Jesus tells us that true happiness comes from none of these things. It is found in God alone. Even our desire to be happy comes from God. He has placed this desire in the hearts of all people.

Jesus' well-known teachings about happiness in the New Testament are called the Beatitudes. (Check out Matthew 5:1–12 in your Bible or appendix B of this handbook.) *Beatitude* is a word that means "happiness" or "blessedness." Jesus shares the Beatitudes as a way of telling us where the life of faith is leading us. Remember, death is not the end for us. God wants our final destination to be Heaven, where we will see God and where our desire for happiness will be completely satisfied. During our lives on earth, the Holy Spirit helps us to make good decisions that keep us on the path to Heaven and true happiness.

© Tischenko Irina/Shutterstock.com

Some material things bring short-term happiness. But riches are not the key to true fulfillment. Where do you find happiness in your daily life?

life is a model for your own—or to use your baptismal name as your Confirmation name. Whichever option you chose, it's time to refresh your memory and recall for yourself why you chose the name you did.

### Receive the Sacrament of Penance and Reconciliation

The Church strongly encourages everyone to celebrate the Sacrament of Penance and Reconciliation before celebrating the Sacrament of Confirmation. Confirmation is a major step in your life as a Christian, so it's good to come to this sacred event totally free of sin. The Church says we have to go to the Sacrament of Penance and Reconciliation and confess our sins only if we are in

When you celebrate Penance and Reconciliation, you receive God's grace and forgiveness. Why is it a good idea to celebrate the Sacrament of Penance and Reconciliation before Confirmation?

## MyMission

### The Final Steps

You are in the final days or weeks before you receive the Sacrament of Confirmation. Your mission is to take the final steps! What do you need to do to be fully ready? Do you need to have a final talk with your sponsor? Do you need to call friends and family members and invite them to come? Have you celebrated the Sacrament of Penance and Reconciliation yet? Write down the things you plan to do between now and the big day.

# Catholic Connection

## The Sacrament of Penance and Reconciliation

We were created for relationship with God. And communion with God is the source of all happiness. Even after Baptism, however, we have a tendency to sin and to weaken our bond with God and the Church. The great news for us is that we have been given Sacraments for the forgiveness of these sins. In the Eucharist, we can ask for and receive forgiveness of our less serious, or venial, sins. But God also provides us with a Sacrament for forgiveness of all our sins—our serious, or mortal, sins as well as our less serious sins. It can be called the Sacrament of conversion, forgiveness, reconciliation, penance, or confession, but its official name is the Sacrament of Penance and Reconciliation.

This Sacrament involves sorrow, confession, penance, and absolution. After we examine our conscience, we confess our sins to a priest. Conversion, which means "change," is central to this Sacrament because it means we are really sorry and willing to change. We are not just confessing our sins so we can go and sin again. Conversion includes true sorrow for our sins and a promise to sin no more.

The priest gives us a penance and absolves us of our sins. A penance is something we do to make up for our sins and some of the hurt they caused. It may also be something that helps us avoid sin in the future. The absolution is the part of the Sacrament when we receive God's forgiveness through the ministry of the priest.

Celebrating the Sacrament of Penance and Reconciliation is an important part of your preparation for Confirmation. It's way more than something you "have to do." It's another free gift from God. It's a gift of forgiveness, love, and grace.

the state of mortal, or serious, sin, but it's a good idea even if our sins are less serious. We confess by telling a priest our sins. We must include our mortal sins, but the Church highly recommends that we confess our venial sins too, so we are better able to live as God wants.

Don't think of the Sacrament of Penance and Reconciliation as a "you have to go" requirement that must be checked off your pre-Confirmation to-do list. Focus on the fact that it is a gift from God, who continually calls us to holiness and showers us with love. It is a gift that restores and strengthens our bond with God—Father, Son, and Holy Spirit—and with the Church.

### Decide What to Wear

Confirmation is one of the biggest days of your life. Make sure you have appropriate clothes clean and ready to wear. Your parish may have a dress code, so be sure you know what it is. There is no need to buy anything new—just dress like it's an important occasion, because it is!

## Rehearsing for the Celebration of Confirmation

Every parish celebrates Confirmation a little differently, and every parish rehearses for Confirmation differently. A parish leader will give you specific details for the rehearsal and celebration of Confirmation, but here is a general overview.

First, you need to know that you can't really "rehearse" receiving grace. The Holy Spirit will be poured out upon you in a way you can't fully imagine! That's part of why we call any sacrament a mystery. We can't fully imagine God's grace and power. So, relax!

## Right from the Rite

"May God the Father almighty bless you, whom he has made his adopted sons and daughters reborn from water and the Holy Spirit, and may he keep you worthy of his fatherly love." (*Order of Confirmation*, number 33)

God is in control. The bishop, your pastor, and the other liturgical ministers will make sure everything goes according to plan. You just need to be there with a loving heart and an open mind.

At the same time, the celebration runs more smoothly if everyone knows where to sit and when to move. Any liturgy, and particularly the Confirmation liturgy, has a certain choreography. You need to know how to respond to the bishop after he anoints you. Pay attention to where you are supposed to be and think about your responses. But don't get uptight about it. Your sponsor will be with you, and it's his or her job to help you do the right thing at the right time.

Knowing the basic outline of the liturgy will help you feel comfortable with what will happen. You may already feel comfortable with the basic outline of the Sacrament of Confirmation because this entire book has followed that outline. Remember, at the beginning of this program, we described how each chapter of this book would correspond to a part of the Order of Confirmation, so, in working through this program, you've already been walking through the rite.

Now, here's a more condensed overview of the Order of Confirmation.

## A Walk Through the Order of Confirmation

### Introductory Rites

Candidates, sponsors, families and other members of the community gather for the celebration. You may be invited, along with your sponsor, to participate in the opening procession with the bishop, parish priests, and the other liturgical ministers. Everyone will stand and sing during the procession.

### Liturgy of the Word

All will hear the Word of God proclaimed. The readings will be those designated for the day on which Confirmation is celebrated, or they will be specially selected from a list of readings suggested in the *Lectionary*.

### Presentation of the Candidates

A leader from the parish will present you and the other candidates to the bishop. Unless the size of the group prevents it, the person making the presentation will call each candidate by name (see chapter 1).

### Homily

The Liturgy of the Word continues with the homily. The bishop's homily will explain the Scripture readings and help everyone

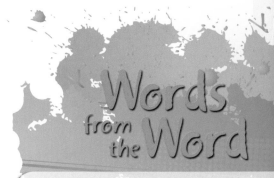

**Words from the Word**

"You will receive power when the holy Spirit comes upon you, and you will be my witnesses in Jerusalem, throughout Judea and Samaria, and to the ends of the earth." (Acts of the Apostles 1:8)

**Dear God**

You have called me to be
    your own son or daughter.
I have answered your call
    and will soon be confirmed.
I am eager to receive the Gifts
    of the Holy Spirit and
    become more like
    Jesus Christ.
I pray that I will come
    to the Sacrament ready
    and open to receive the
    fullness of your Spirit.
In Jesus' name I ask
    these things.
Amen.

to gain a better understanding of the meaning and significance of the Sacrament of Confirmation (see chapter 1).

## Renewal of Baptismal Promises

Remember those promises made at your Baptism? Remember how we talked about those back in chapter 3? Well, here is where they come in. Before the bishop seals your Baptism and confirms your faith, he asks you to renew those promises. The renewal of those promises helps to express the close connection between Baptism and Confirmation. The response, a series of "I do's," may appear simple, but the meaning is all important. You and the other candidates are asked to denounce Satan and profess belief in God—Father, Son, and Holy Spirit. You all will listen to the questions and then loudly and clearly answer, "I do."

## The Laying On of Hands

The bishop and the priests lay hands upon you and all the candidates by extending their hands over the whole group (see chapter 4). This gesture signifies the gift of the Holy Spirit. The bishop calls upon the Father in prayer, asking that he send the Holy Spirit upon all the candidates. Can you name the seven Gifts of the Holy Spirit, which are named in this prayer (see chapter 5)?

## The Anointing with Sacred Chrism

This is the heart of the Sacrament of Confirmation (see chapter 6). Your sponsor will place her or his right hand on your shoulder as a sign of support and commitment to helping you live faithfully. She or he will present you to the bishop by telling him the name you've chosen. Then the bishop will repeat your name and anoint you. He will make the Sign of the Cross on your forehead while saying, "Be sealed with the gift of the Holy Spirit" (*Order of Confirmation*, number 27). You will respond, "Amen," and then exchange words of peace with the bishop. This is the dialogue between you and the bishop:

**Bishop:** *(Your name)*,
be sealed with the Gift
of the Holy Spirit.
**You:** Amen.
**Bishop:** Peace be with you.
**You:** And with your Spirit.
(*Order of Confirmation*, number 27)

© Bill Wittman

Notice the elements of Confirmation shown here: the anointing, the bishop as minister of Confirmation, the sponsor with his hand on the shoulder. What else do you notice?

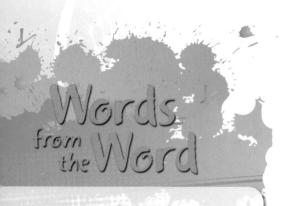

## Words from the Word

"I will pour out my Spirit on everyone:

your sons and daughters will proclaim my message;

your old people will have dreams, and your young people will see visions."

(Joel 2:28, GNT)

This exchange of peace between the bishop and the candidates is a sign of the bond or close relationship the faithful have with one another and with the bishop.

### The General Intercessions

After everyone has been anointed, the community will join together in prayer. Everyone responds, "Lord, hear our prayer," or something similar.

### The Liturgy of the Eucharist

When the Sacrament of Confirmation is celebrated within the Mass, which is typical, the celebration continues with the Liturgy of the Eucharist. This helps to highlight the unity of the three Sacraments of Initiation and the communion among all the people with God. At the end of the Mass, everyone is sent forth to love and serve the Lord.

## After Confirmation

The celebrating will probably continue in the parish hall or some other place where you may have a chance to speak with the bishop, or you might go back to your house or out to dinner. Whatever you do to continue celebrating, remember that Confirmation is a beginning—the beginning of your life as a fully initiated Catholic.

# The Big Event: It's Almost Here!

The celebration of Confirmation is a big deal. You will receive the outpouring of the Holy Spirit. What is the significance of the gift of the Holy Spirit being given to you in Confirmation? What does it mean to become a full member of the Church? What does it mean to be bound more closely to the Church and to Christ?

# Appendix A
## Catholic Prayers

### Act of Contrition

My God, I am sorry for my sins
with all my heart, and I detest them.
In choosing to do wrong and failing to do
good,
I have sinned against you,
whom I should love above all things.
I firmly intend, with your help,
to do penance, to sin no more,
and to avoid whatever leads me to sin.
Our savior Jesus Christ suffered and died for
us.
In his name, my God, have mercy.

### Act of Faith

My God, I firmly believe you are one God
in three Divine Persons, Father, Son, and
Holy Spirit.
I believe in Jesus Christ, your Son, who
became man and died for our sins, and
who will come to
judge the living and the dead.
I believe these and all the truths which the
Holy Catholic Church teaches, because
you have revealed them, who can neither
deceive nor be deceived.
Amen.

## Act of Hope

O my God, trusting in your infinite goodness and promises, I hope to obtain pardon of my sins, the help of your grace, and life everlasting, through the merits of Jesus Christ, my Lord and redeemer. Amen.

## Act of Love

My God, I love you above all things, with my whole heart and soul, because you are all-good and worthy of all my love. I love my neighbor as myself for love of you. I forgive all who have injured me, and I ask pardon of all whom I have injured. Amen.

## Angelus

The angel of the Lord declared unto Mary,
And she conceived of the Holy Spirit.
　　Hail Mary . . .
Behold the handmaid of the Lord,
Be it done unto me according to your word.
　　Hail Mary . . .
And the Word was made flesh,
And dwelt among us.
　　Hail Mary . . .
Pray for us, O Holy Mother of God, that we may be made worthy of the promises of Christ. Let us pray: Pour forth, we beseech you, O Lord, your grace into our hearts that we to whom the incarnation of Christ, your Son, was made known by the message of the angel may, by his passion and cross, be brought to the glory of his resurrection, through Christ our Lord.

## Apostles' Creed

I believe in God, the Father almighty, Creator of heaven and earth, and in Jesus Christ, his only Son, our Lord, who was conceived by the Holy Spirit, born of the Virgin Mary, suffered under Pontius Pilate, was crucified, died and was buried; he descended into hell; on the third day he rose again from the dead; he ascended into heaven, and is seated at the right hand of God the Father almighty; from there he will come to judge the living and the dead.

I believe in the Holy Spirit, the holy catholic Church, the communion of saints, the forgiveness of sins, the resurrection of the body, and life everlasting. Amen.

## Blessing of Chrism

God our maker,
source of all growth in holiness,
accept the joyful thanks and praise
we offer in the name of your Church.

In the beginning, at your command,
the earth produced fruit-bearing trees.
From the fruit of the olive tree
you have provided us with oil for holy chrism.
The prophet David sang of the life and joy
that the oil would bring us in the sacraments
    of your love.

After the avenging flood,
the dove returning to Noah with an olive
    branch
announced your gift of peace.
This was a sign of a greater gift to come.
Now the waters of baptism wash away the
    sins of men,
and by the anointing with olive oil
you make us radiant with your joy.

At your command,
Aaron was washed with water,

and our servant Moses, his brother,
anointed him priest.
This too foreshadowed greater things to
    come.
After your Son, Jesus Christ our Lord,
asked John for baptism in the waters of
    Jordan,
you sent the Spirit upon him
in the form of a dove
and by the witness of your own voice
you declared him to be your only, well-
    beloved Son.
In this you clearly fulfilled the prophecy of
    David,
that Christ would be anointed with the oil of
    gladness
beyond his fellow men.

And so, Father, we ask you to bless this oil
    you have created.

Fill it with the power of your Holy Spirit
through Christ your Son.
It is from him that chrism takes its name
and with chrism you have anointed
for yourself priests and kings,
prophets and martyrs.

Make this chrism a sign of life and salvation
for those who are to be born again in the
    waters of baptism.
Wash away the evil they have inherited from
    sinful Adam,
And when they are anointed with this holy oil
make them temples of your glory,
radiant with the goodness of life
that has its source in you.

Through this sign of chrism
Grant them royal, priestly, and prophetic
    honor,

and clothe them with incorruption.
Let this be indeed the chrism of salvation
for those who will be born again of water
    and the Holy Spirit.
May they come to share eternal life
in the glory of your kingdom.
We ask this through Christ our Lord
Amen.

## *Confiteor* (I Confess)

I confess to almighty God and to you, my brothers and sisters, that I have greatly sinned in my thoughts and in my words, in what I have done and in what I have failed to do, through my fault, through my fault, through my most grievous fault; therefore I ask blessed Mary ever-Virgin, all the Angels and Saints, and you, my brothers and sisters, to pray for me to the Lord our God.

## Glory Be

Glory be to the Father, and to the Son, and to the Holy Spirit, as it was in the beginning, is now, and will be forever. Amen.

## Grace Before Meals

Bless us, O Lord, and these your gifts,
which we are about to receive
from your bounty,
through Christ our Lord. Amen.

## Grace After Meals

We give you thanks, almighty God,
for these and all your gifts
which we have received
through Christ our Lord. Amen.

## Hail Mary

Hail Mary, full of grace,
the Lord is with you;
blessed are you among women,
and blessed is the fruit of your womb, Jesus.

Holy Mary, Mother of God,
pray for us sinners
now and at the hour of our death.
Amen.

## Lord's Prayer (Our Father)

Our Father who art in heaven,
hallowed be thy name.
Thy kingdom come.
Thy will be done on earth, as it is in heaven.
Give us this day our daily bread,
and forgive us our trespasses,
as we forgive those who trespass against us,
and lead us not into temptation,
but deliver us from evil. Amen.

## *Magnificat* (Mary's Song) (See Luke 1:46–55)

My being proclaims the greatness of the
   Lord,
my spirit finds joy in God my savior.
For he has looked upon his servant
in all her lowliness.
All ages to come shall call me blessed.
God who is mighty
has done great things for me, holy is his
   name;
his mercy is from age to age
on those who fear him.
He has shown might with his arm;
he has confused the proud
in their inmost thoughts.
He has deposed the mighty from their thrones

and raised the lowly to high places.
The hungry he has given every good thing
while the rich he has sent empty away.
He has upheld Israel his servant,
ever mindful of his mercy,
even as he promised our fathers,
promised Abraham and his descendants
forever.

## Memorare

Remember, O most gracious Virgin Mary, that never was it known that anyone who fled to your protection, implored your help, or sought your intercession was left unaided. Inspired by this confidence, we fly unto you, O virgin of virgins, our mother. To you do we come, before you we stand, sinful and sorrowful. O mother of the Word Incarnate, despise not our petitions, but in your mercy, hear and answer us.

## Morning Prayer

Almighty God, I thank you for your past blessings. Today I offer myself—whatever I do, say, or think—to your loving care. Continue to bless me, Lord. I make this morning offering in union with the divine intentions of Jesus Christ who offers himself daily in the holy sacrifice of the Mass, and in union with Mary, his Virgin Mother and our Mother, who was always the faithful handmaid of the Lord. Amen.

## Nicene Creed

I believe in one God, the Father almighty, maker of heaven and earth, of all things visible and invisible.

I believe in one Lord Jesus Christ, the Only Begotten Son of God, born of the Father before all ages. God from God, Light from Light, true God from true God, begotten, not made, consubstantial with the Father; through him all things were made. For us men and for our salvation he came down from heaven, and by the Holy Spirit was incarnate of the Virgin Mary, and became man.

For our sake he was crucified under Pontius Pilate, he suffered death and was buried, and rose again on the third day in accordance with the Scriptures. He ascended into heaven and is seated at the right hand of the Father. He will come again in glory to judge the living and the dead and his kingdom will have no end.

I believe in the Holy Spirit, the Lord, the giver of life, who proceeds from the Father and the Son, who with the Father and the Son is adored and glorified, who has spoken through the prophets.

I believe in one, holy, catholic and apostolic Church. I confess one Baptism for the forgiveness of sins and I look forward to the resurrection of the dead and the life of the world to come. Amen.

## Prayer of Saint Francis

Lord, make me an instrument of your peace:
    where there is hatred, let me sow love;
    where there is injury, pardon;
    where there is doubt, faith;
    where there is despair, hope;
    where there is darkness, light;
    where there is sadness, joy.
Divine Master,
    grant that I may not so much seek
    to be consoled as to console,
    to be understood as to understand,
    to be loved as to love.
For it is in giving that we receive,
    it is in pardoning that we are pardoned,
    it is in dying that we are born to eternal life.

## Prayer to the Holy Spirit

Come, Holy Spirit, fill the hearts of your faithful. Enkindle in them the fire of your love. Send forth your Spirit, and they will be created. And you will renew the face of the earth.

Let us pray:

Lord, by the light of the Holy Spirit, you have taught the hearts of the faithful. In the same Spirit, help us to relish what is right and always rejoice in your consolation. We ask this through Christ our Lord. Amen.

## Renewal of Baptismal Promises (*Order of Confirmation,* number 23)

**Bishop:** Do you renounce Satan, and all his works and empty promises?

**Candidates:** I do.

**Bishop:** Do you believe in God, the Father almighty, Creator of heaven and earth?

**Candidates:** I do.

**Bishop:** Do you believe in Jesus Christ, his only Son, our Lord, who was born of the Virgin Mary, suffered death and was buried, rose again from the dead and is seated at the right hand of the Father?

**Candidates:** I do.

**Bishop:** Do you believe in the Holy Spirit, the Lord, the giver of life, who today through the Sacrament of Confirmation is given to you in a special way just as he was given to the Apostles on the day of Pentecost?

**Candidates:** I do.

**Bishop:** Do you believe in the holy Catholic Church, the communion of saints, the forgiveness of sins, the resurrection of the body, and life everlasting?

**Candidates:** I do.

# Rosary

The Rosary is perhaps the most popular devotion to Mary, the Mother of God. The central part of the Rosary consists of the recitation of five sets of ten Hail Marys (each set is called a decade). Each new decade begins by saying an Our Father, and each decade concludes with a Glory Be. Individuals keep track of the prayers said by moving from one bead to the next in order.

The recitation of the Rosary begins with a series of prayers, said in the following order while using as a guide a small chain of beads and a crucifix:

1. the Sign of the Cross
2. the Apostles' Creed
3. one Our Father
4. three Hail Marys
5. one Glory Be

After these introductory prayers, the recitation of the decades begins.

The saying of a five-decade Rosary is connected with meditation on what are called the mysteries of the life of Jesus. These mysteries too are collected into series of five—five joyful, five luminous, five sorrowful, and five glorious mysteries. Individuals who are praying devote one recitation of the Rosary to each set of mysteries. They choose which set of mysteries to meditate on while saying the decades of Hail Marys. Therefore, the *complete* Rosary consists of twenty decades.

With a little practice, the regular praying of the Rosary can become a source of great inspiration and consolation for Christians.

## Joyful Mysteries

- The Annunciation
- The Visitation
- The Birth of Our Lord
- The Presentation of Jesus in the Temple
- The Finding of Jesus in the Temple

### Mysteries of Light

- The Baptism of Jesus
- Jesus Reveals Himself in the Miracle at Cana
- Jesus Proclaims the Good News of the Kingdom of God
- The Transfiguration of Jesus
- The Institution of the Eucharist

### Sorrowful Mysteries

- The Agony of Jesus in the Garden
- The Scourging at the Pillar
- The Crowning of Thorns
- The Carrying of the Cross
- The Crucifixion

### Glorious Mysteries

- The Resurrection of Jesus
- The Ascension of Jesus into Heaven
- The Descent of the Holy Spirit on the Apostles (Pentecost)
- The Assumption of Mary into Heaven
- The Crowning of Mary as Queen of Heaven

## Sign of the Cross

In the name of the Father, and of the Son, and of the Holy Spirit. Amen.

## Stations of the Cross

1. Jesus is condemned to death.
2. Jesus takes up his cross.
3. Jesus falls the first time.
4. Jesus meets his mother.
5. Simon helps Jesus carry the cross.
6. Veronica wipes the face of Jesus.
7. Jesus falls the second time.
8. Jesus meets the women of Jerusalem.

9. Jesus falls the third time.

10. Jesus is stripped of his garments.

11. Jesus is nailed to the cross.

12. Jesus dies on the cross.

13. Jesus is taken down from the cross.

14. Jesus is laid in the tomb.

# Appendix B
## Catholic Beliefs and Practices

This section provides brief summaries of major Catholic beliefs and practices.

### Two Great Commandments (See Matthew 22:37–40, Mark 12:29–31, Luke 10:27)

- You shall love the Lord your God with all your heart, with all your soul, and all your mind, and with all your strength.
- You shall love your neighbor as yourself.

### Ten Commandments

1. I am the Lord your God: you shall not have strange gods before me.
2. You shall not take the name of the Lord, your God, in vain.
3. Remember to keep holy the Lord's Day.
4. Honor your father and mother.
5. You shall not kill.
6. You shall not commit adultery.
7. You shall not steal.
8. You shall not bear false witness against your neighbor.
9. You shall not covet your neighbor's wife.
10. You shall not covet your neighbor's goods.

## Beatitudes (Matthew 5:3–10)

- Blessed are the poor in spirit, for theirs is the kingdom of heaven.
- Blessed are they who mourn, for they will be comforted.
- Blessed are the meek, for they will inherit the land.
- Blessed are they who hunger and thirst for righteousness, for they will be satisfied.
- Blessed are the merciful, for they will be shown mercy.
- Blessed are the clean of heart, for they will see God.
- Blessed are the peacemakers, for they will be called children of God.
- Blessed are they who are persecuted for the sake of righteousness, for theirs is the kingdom of heaven.

## Corporal Works of Mercy

- Feed the hungry.
- Give drink to the thirsty.
- Shelter the homeless.
- Clothe the naked.
- Care for the sick.
- Help the imprisoned.
- Bury the dead.

## Spiritual Works of Mercy

- Share knowledge.
- Give advice to those who need it.
- Comfort those who suffer.
- Be patient with others.
- Forgive those who hurt you.
- Give correction to those who need it.
- Pray for the living and the dead.

## Theological Virtues

- Faith
- Hope
- Love

## Cardinal Virtues

- Prudence
- Justice
- Fortitude
- Temperance

## Seven Gifts of the Holy Spirit (See chapter 5)

- **Wisdom.** A wise person recognizes where the Holy Spirit is at work in the world.
- **Understanding.** Understanding helps us to recognize how God wants us to live.
- **Counsel (right judgment).** This gift helps us to make choices that will lead us closer to God rather than away from God. The gift of counsel, or right judgment, helps us to figure out what God wants.
- **Fortitude (courage).** The gift of fortitude, also called courage, is the special help we need when faced with challenges or struggles.
- **Knowledge.** This gift helps us to understand the meaning of what God has revealed, particularly the Good News of Jesus Christ.
- **Piety (Reverence).** This gift of piety or reverence gives us a deep sense of respect for God and the Church. A reverent person honors God and approaches him with humility, trust, and love.
- **Fear of the Lord (wonder and awe).** The gift of fear of the Lord makes us aware of God's greatness and power.

## Fruits of the Holy Spirit (See chapter 5)

- Charity
- Joy
- Peace
- Patience
- Kindness
- Goodness
- Generosity (or long suffering)
- Gentleness (or humility)
- Faithfulness
- Modesty
- Self-control (or continence)
- Chastity

## Four Marks of the Catholic Church

- One
- Holy
- Catholic
- Apostolic

## Liturgical Year

- Advent
- Christmas
- Ordinary Time
- Lent
- Easter Triduum
- Easter
- Pentecost
- Ordinary Time

## Seven Sacraments

- Baptism
- Confirmation
- the Eucharist
- Penance and Reconciliation
- Anointing of the Sick
- Matrimony
- Holy Orders

## Precepts of the Church

- Keep holy Sundays and holy days of obligation and attend Mass on these days.
- Confess your sins in the Sacrament of Penance and Reconciliation at least once a year.
- Receive Communion at least during the Easter season.
- Follow the Church's rules concerning fasting and abstaining from eating meat.
- Strengthen and support the Church by providing for the material needs of the Church according to your ability.

## Holy Days of Obligation

- Christmas (December 25)
- Solemnity of the Blessed Virgin Mary, the Mother of God (January 1)
- Ascension of the Lord (the Thursday that falls on the fortieth day after Easter, though in some places the celebration is moved to the following Sunday)
- Assumption of the Blessed Virgin Mary (August 15)
- All Saints (November 1)
- Immaculate Conception of the Blessed Virgin Mary (December 8)

## Parts of the Mass

Introductory Rites
- Entrance Chant
- Greeting
- Penitential Act
- *Kyrie*
- Gloria
- Collect (opening prayer)

Liturgy of the Word
- First Reading
- Responsorial Psalm

- Second Reading
- Gospel Acclamation
- Gospel Reading
- Homily
- Profession of Faith
- Prayer of the Faithful

Liturgy of the Eucharist
- Presentation and Preparation of the Gifts
- Prayer over the Offerings
- Eucharistic Prayer
- Communion Rite:
  - Lord's Prayer
  - Sign of Peace
  - Lamb of God
  - Communion
  - Prayer after Communion

Concluding Rites
- Prayer over the People
- Final Blessing
- Dismissal

# Appendix C

## Patron Saints and Their Causes

### A

**Accountants,** Saint Matthew, *September 21*

**Actors,** Saint Genesius, *August 25*

**Addicts,** Saint Maximilian Maria Kolbe, *August 14*

**Advertising,** Saint Bernardino of Siena, *May 20*

**African-Americans,** Saint Benedict the African, *April 4;* Saint Martin de Porres, *November 3;* Saint Peter Claver, *September 9*

**AIDS patients,** Saint Peregrine Laziosi, *May 16*

**Air travelers,** Saint Joseph of Cupertino, *September 18*

**Alcoholics,** Venerable Matt Talbot; Saint Monica, *August 27*

**Altar servers,** Saint John Berchmans, *November 26*

**Americas,** Our Lady of Guadalupe, *December 12;* Saint Rose of Lima, *August 23*

**Blacksmiths,** Saint Dunstan,
May 19

**Blindness,** Raphael (Michael, Gabriel, and Raphael), *September 29;* Saint Lucy, *December 13*

**Bodily ills,** Our Lady of Lourdes,
*February 11*

**Bohemia,** Saint Wenceslaus,
*September 28*

**Bookkeepers,** Saint Matthew, *September 21*

**Booksellers,** Saint John of God,
*March 8*

**Boy Scouts,** Saint George, *April 23*

**Boys,** Saint John Bosco, *January 31*

**Brazil,** Saint Peter of Alcántara, *October 22;* Saint Anthony of Padua, *June 13*

**Breast disease, against,** Saint Agatha, *February 5*

**Brewers,** Saint Augustine of Hippo, *August 28;* Saint Luke, *October 18;* Saint Nicholas of Myra, *December 6*

**Bricklayers,** Saint Stephen,
*August 16*

**Brides**, Saint Nicholas of Myra,
*December 6*

**Broadcasters,** Saint Gabriel, *September 29*

**Builders,** Saint Barbara, *December 4;* Saint Vincent Ferrer, *April 5*

**Businessmen,** Saint Homobonus,
*November 13*

**Businesswomen,** Saint Margaret Clitherow, *March 26*

**Butchers,** Saint Anthony the Abbot, *January 17;* Saint Luke, *October 18*

## C

**Cab drivers,** Saint Fiacre,
*August 30*

**Canada,** Saints Ann and Joachim, *July 26;* Saint Joseph, *March 19*

**Cancer patients,** Saint Peregrine Laziosi, *May 16*

**Carpenters,** Saint Joseph, *March 19*

**Catechists,** Saint Charles Borromeo, *November 4*; Saint Robert Bellarmine, *September 17*; Saint Viator, *December 14*

**Catechumens,** Saint Charles Borromeo, *November 4*; Saint Robert Bellarmine, *September 17*

**Catholic schools,** Saint Thomas Aquinas, *January 28*

**Catholic youth,** Saint Aloysius Gonzaga, *June 21*; Saint Maria Goretti, *July 6*

**Charities,** Saint Vincent de Paul, *September 27*

**Childbirth,** Saint Gerard Majella, *October 16*; Saint Raymond Nonnatus, *August 31*

**Children,** Saint Nicholas, *December 6*

**Chile,** Our Lady of Mount Carmel, *July 16*; Saint James the Greater, *July 25*

**China,** Saint Joseph, *March 19*

**Choirboys,** Saint Dominic Savio, *March 9*

**Church,** Saint Joseph, *March 19*

**Civil servants,** Saint Thomas More, *June 22*

**Clergy,** Saint Gabriel of Our Lady of Sorrows, *September 15*

**Colleges,** Saint Thomas Aquinas, *January 28*

**Colombia,** Saint Louis Bertrand, *October 9*; Saint Peter Claver, *September 9*

**Comedians,** Saint Vitus, *June 15*

**Communication workers,** Saint Gabriel, *September 29*

**Computers,** Saint Isidore of Seville, *April 4*

**Construction workers,** Saint Thomas the Apostle, *July 3*

**Cooks,** Saint Lawrence, *August 10*; Saint Thomas the Apostle, *July 3*

**Court clerks,** Saint Thomas More, *June 22*

## D

**Dairy workers,** Saint Brigid of Kildare, *February 1*

**Dancers,** Saint Vitus, *June 15*

**Deacons,** Saint Stephen, *December 26*

**Deafness,** Saint Francis de Sales, *January 24*

**Death,** Saint Joseph, *March 19*; Saint Michael, *September 29*

**Denmark,** Saint Ansgar, *February 3*; Saint Canute, *January 19*

**Dentists,** Saint Apollonia, *February 9*

**Desperate causes,** Saint Jude (Simon and Jude), *October 28*

**Difficult marriages,** Saint Rita of Cascia, *May 22*

**Disabilities,** Saint Giles, *September 1*

**Disasters,** Saint Genevieve, *January 3*

**Doctors,** Saint Luke, *October 18*

**Dogs,** Saint Roch, *August 16*

**Domestic workers,** Saint Zita of Lucca, *April 27*

**Dominican Republic,** Saint Dominic, *August 8*

**Drivers,** Saint Fiacre, *August 30*

**Drug addiction,** Saint Maximilian Mary Kolbe, *August 14*

## E

**Earaches,** Saint Polycarp, *February 23*

**Earthquakes,** Saint Francis Borgia, *October 10*

**Ecology,** Saint Francis of Assisi, *October 4*

**Editors,** Saint John Bosco, *January 31*

**Engineers,** Saint Patrick, *March 17*; Saint Ferdinand III, *May 30*

**England,** Saint Augustine of Canterbury, *May 17*; Saint George, *April 23*; Saint Gregory the Great, *September 3*

**Epilepsy,** Saint Dymphna, *May 30;* Saint Vitus, *June 15;* Saint Willibrord, *November 7*

**Europe,** Saint Benedict, *July 11;* Saint Bridget, *February 1;* Saint Catherine of Siena, *April 29*

**Eye disorders,** Saint Clare, *August 11;* Saint Lucy, *December 13*

# F

**Falsely accused,** Saint Raymond Nonnatus, *August 31*

**Farmers,** Saint Isidore the Farmer, *May 15*

**Fathers,** Saint Joseph, *March 19*

**Firefighters,** Saint Florian, *May 4;* Saint John of God, *March 8*

**Fishermen,** Saint Andrew, *November 30;* Saint Peter (Peter and Paul), *June 29*

**Florists,** Saint Thérèse of Lisieux, *October 1;* Saint Rose of Lima, *August 23;* Saint Dorothy, *February 6*

**Foundry workers,** Saint Agatha, *February 5*

**France,** Our Lady of the Assumption, *August 15;* Saint Denis, *October 9;* Saint Joan of Arc, *May 30*

**Funeral directors,** Saint Joan of Arc, *May 30*

# G

**Gambling, compulsive,** Saint Bernardine of Siena, *May 20*

**Gardeners,** Saint Adelard, *January 2;* Saint Fiacre, *August 30*

**Germany,** Saint Boniface, *June 5;* Saint George, *April 23;* Saint Michael, *September 29;* Saint Peter Canisius, *December 21*

**Girls,** Saint Agnes, *January 21;* Saint Maria Goretti, *July 6*

**Grandparents,** Saints Ann and Joachim, *July 26*

**Gravediggers,** Saint Anthony the Abbot, *January 17*

**Greece,** Saint Andrew, *November 30*; Saint Nicholas, *December 6*

**Greetings,** Saint Valentine, *February 14*

**Grocers,** Saint Michael, *September 29*

**Grooms,** Saint Louis of France, *August 25*; Saint Nicholas, *December 6*

# H

**Hairdressers,** Saint Martin de Porres, *November 3*

**Happy death,** Saint Joseph, *March 19*

**Headaches,** Saint Teresa of Ávila, *October 15*

**Heart patients,** Saint John of God, *March 8*

**Homeless,** Saint Benedict, *July 11*; Joseph Labre, *April 17*

**Horses,** Saint Martin of Tours, *November 11*

**Hospital administrators,** Saint Frances Xavier Cabrini, *November 13*

**Hospitals,** Saint Camillus de Lellis, *July 14*; Saint John of God, *March 8*

**Hotel keepers,** Saint Amand, *February 6*

**Housewives,** Saints Ann and Joachim, *July 26*; Saint Martha, *July 29*

**Hungary,** Saint Gerard, *September 24*; Saint Stephen, *August 16*

**Hunters,** Saint Hubert, *November 3*; Saint Eustachius, *September 20*

# I

**Immigrants,** Saint Frances Xavier Cabrini, *November 13*

**Impossible causes,** Saint Frances Xavier Cabrini, *November 13*; Saint Rita of Cascia, *May 22*

**India,** Our Lady of the Assumption, *August 15*

**Infertility,** Saint Philomena, *August 11*; Saint Rita of Cascia, *May 22*

**Insanity,** Saint Dymphna, *May 30*

**Internet,** Saint Isidore of Seville, *April 4*

**Invalids,** Saint Roch, *August 16*

**Ireland,** Saint Brigid of Kildare, *February 1*; Saint Columba, *June 9*; Saint Patrick, *March 17*

**Italy,** Saint Bernardine of Siena, *May 20*; Saint Catherine of Siena, *April 29*; Saint Francis of Assisi, *October 4*

## J

**Japan,** Saint Francis Xavier, *December 3*; Saint Peter Baptist and Companions, *February 6*

**Jewelers,** Saint Eligius, *December 1*

**Jordan,** Saint John the Baptist, *February 6*

**Journalists,** Saint Francis de Sales, *January 24*

**Judges,** Saint John of Capistrano, *October 23*

**Juvenile delinquents,** Saint Dominic Savio, *March 9*

## K

**Kidney disease,** Saint Benedict, *July 11*

**Knee problems,** Saint Roch, *August 16*

## L

**Laborers,** Saint Isidore the Farmer, *May 15*; Saint James the Greater, *July 25*

**Latin America,** Saint Rose of Lima, *August 23*

**Lawyers,** Saint Raymond of Penyafort, *January 7*; Saint Thomas More, *June 22*

**Learning,** Saint Ambrose, *December 7*

**Librarians,** Saint Jerome, *September 30*

**Lithuania,** Saint Casimir, *March 4*

**Longevity,** Saint Peter (Peter and Paul), *June 29*

**Loss of parents,** Saint Elizabeth Ann Seton, *January 24*

**Lost items,** Saint Anthony of Padua, *June 13*

**Lovers,** Saint Valentine, *February 14*

# M

**Married women,** Saint Monica, *August 27*

**Medical technicians,** Saint Albert the Great, *November 15*

**Mentally ill,** Saint Dymphna, *May 30*

**Merchants,** Saint Francis of Assisi, *October 4*; Saint Nicholas, *December 6*

**Messengers,** Saint Gabriel, *September 29*

**Metal workers,** Saint Eligius, *December 1*

**Mexico,** Our Lady of Guadalupe, *December 12*

**Midwives,** Saint Raymond Nonnatus, *August 31*

**Military members,** Saint Joan of Arc, *May 30*

**Miscarriage, prevention of,** Saint Catherine of Sweden, *March 24*

**Missionaries,** Saint Francis Xavier, *December 3*; Saint Thérèse of Lisieux, *October 1*

**Monks,** Saint John the Baptist, *June 24*

**Mothers,** Saint Monica, *August 27*

**Motorists,** Saint Frances of Rome, *March 9*

**Musicians,** Saint Cecilia, *November 22*

**Mystics,** Saint John of the Cross, *December 14*

## N

**Netherlands,** Saint Willibrord, *November 7*

**Neurological diseases,** Saint Dymphna, *May 30*

**New Zealand,** Our Lady Help of Christians, *May 24*

**Nicaragua,** Saint James the Greater, *July 25*

**Nigeria,** Saint Patrick, *March 17*

**North Africa,** Saint Cyprian, *September 16*

**North America,** Saint Isaac Jogues, *October 19*; John de Brébeuf and Companions, *October 19*

**Norway,** Saint Olaf, *July 29*

**Notaries,** Saint Luke, *October 18*; Saint Mark, *April 25*

**Nuns,** Saint Brigid of Kildare, *February 1*; Saint Scholastica, *February 10*

**Nurses,** Saint Agatha, *February 5*; Saint Camillus de Lellis, *July 14*; Saint John of God, *March 8*

## O

**Obstetricians,** Saint Raymond Nonnatus, *August 31*

**Oceania,** Saint Peter Chanel, *April 28*

**Orators,** Saint John Chrysostom, *September 13*

**Orphans, abandoned children,** Saint Jerome Emiliani, *February 8*

## P

**Painters,** Saint Luke, *October 18*

**Paraguay,** Our Lady of the Assumption, *August 15*

**Paralysis,** Saint Osmund,
*December 4*

**Parenthood,** Saint Rita of Cascia,
*May 22*

**Parish priests,** Saint John Vianney,
*August 4*

**Pawnbrokers,** Saint Nicholas,
*December 6*

**Penitents,** Saint Mary Magdalene,
*July 22*

**Perfumers,** Saint Mary Magdalene,
*July 22*

**Peru,** Saint Joseph, *March 19*; Saint
Rose of Lima, *August 23*

**Pharmacists,** Saints Cosmas and
Damian, *September 26*

**Philippines,** Saint Rose of Lima,
*August 23*

**Philosophers,** Saint Albert the
Great, *November 15*; Saint Catherine of Alexandria, *November 25*

**Physicians,** Saints Cosmas and
Damian, *September 26*; Saint Luke,
*October 18*

**Pilots,** Saint Joseph of Cupertino,
*September 18*; Saint Thérèse of
Lisieux, *October 1*

**Poets,** Saint Columba, *June 9*; Saint
David of Wales, *March 1*

**Poisoning,** Saint Benedict, *July 11*

**Poland,** Saint Casimir, *March 4*;
Saint Florian, *May 4*; Saint Stanis-
laus, *November 13*

**Police officers,** Saint Michael,
*September 29*

**Politicians, public servants,**
Saint Thomas More, *June 22*

**Popes,** Saint Peter (Peter and Paul),
*June 29*

**Portugal,** Saint George, *April 23*

**Postal workers,** Saint Gabriel,
*September 29*

**Poverty,** Saint Anthony of Padua,
*June 13*; Saint Lawrence,
*August 10*

**Preachers,** Saint John Chrysostom,
*September 13*

**Pregnant women,** Saints Ann and Joachim, *July 26*; Saint Gerard Majella, *October 16*; Saint Margaret, *July 20*; Saint Raymond Nonnatus, *August 31*

**Priests,** Saint John Vianney, *August 4*

**Printers,** Saint Augustine, *August 28*; Saint John of God, *March 8*

**Prisoners,** Saint Dismas, *March 28*; Saint Joseph Cafasso, *June 23*

**Prussia,** Saint Joseph Cafasso, *June 23*

**Public relations,** Saint Bernardine of Siena, *May 20*

## R

**Race relations,** Saint Martin de Porres, *November 3*

**Radio,** Saint Gabriel, *September 29*

**Radiologists,** Saints Michael, Gabriel, and Raphael, *September 29*

**Reconciliation,** Saint Vincent Ferrer, *April 5*

**Retreats,** Saint Ignatius of Loyola, *July 31*

**Rheumatism,** Saint James the Greater, *July 25*

**Robbers, danger from,** Saint Leonard of Noblac, *November 6*

**Rome,** Saint Peter (Peter and Paul), *June 29*

**Russia,** Saint Andrew, *November 30*; Saint Basil the Great, *January 2*; Saint Casimir, *March 4*; Saint Joseph, *March 19*; Saint Nicholas, *December 6*

## S

**Sailors,** Saint Brendan, *May 16*; Saint Elmo, *June 2*; Saint Francis of Paola, *April 2*

**Savings,** Saint Anthony Claret, *October 24*

**Scholars,** Saint Bede the Venerable, *May 25*; Saint Brigid of Kildare, *February 1*

**Schoolchildren,** Saint Benedict, *July 11*

**Schools,** Saint Thomas Aquinas, *January 28*

**Scientists,** Saint Albert the Great, *November 15*

**Scotland,** Saint Andrew, *November 30*; Saint Margaret, *November 16*

**Sculptors,** Saint Claude, *February 15*

**Secretaries,** Saint Genesius, *August 25*

**Seminarians,** Saint Charles Borromeo, *November 4*

**Serbia,** Saint Sava, *January 14*

**Servants,** Saint Sava, *January 14*; Saint Zita of Lucca, *April 27*

**Shepherds,** Saint Marie Bernadette Soubirous, *April 16*; Saint Paschal Baylon, *May 17*

**Sickness,** Saint John of God, *March 8*

**Skin diseases,** Saint Anthony the Abbot, *January 17*

**Slavic peoples,** Saints Cyril and Methodius, *February 14*

**Sobriety,** Venerable Matt Talbot, *June 7*

**Social justice,** Saint Joseph, *March 19*; Saint Martin de Porres, *November 3*

**Social workers,** Saint Louise de Marillac, *March 15*

**Soldiers,** Saint George, *April 23*; Saint Martin of Tours, *November 11*

**South Africa,** Our Lady of the Assumption, *August 15*

**South America,** Saint Rose of Lima, *August 23*

**Spain,** Saint James the Greater, *July 2*

**Stomach disorders,** Saints Timothy and Titus, *January 26*

**Students,** Saint Catherine of Alexandria, *November 25*; Saint Thomas Aquinas, *January 28*

**Surgeons,** Saints Cosmas and Damian, *September 26*; Saint Luke, *October 18*

**Sweden,** Saint Bridget of Sweden, *July 23*

**Switzerland,** Saint Nicholas von Flue, *March 21*

# T

**Tailors,** Saint Homobonus, *November 13*

**Tax collectors,** Saint Matthew, *September 21*

**Taxi drivers,** Saint Fiacre, *August 30*

**Teachers,** Saint Gregory the Great, *September 3*; Saint John Baptist de La Salle, *April 7*

**Teenagers,** Saint Aloysius Gonzaga, *June 21*; Saint Maria Goretti, *July 6*

**Telecommunications,** Saint Gabriel, *September 29*

**Television,** Saint Clare, *August 11*

**Theologians,** Saint Alphonsus Liguori, *August 1*; Saint Augustine of Hippo, *August 28*

**Throat ailments,** Saint Blase, *February 3*

**Toothache,** Saint Apollonia, *February 9*

**Travelers,** Anthony of Padua, *June 13*

**Turkey,** Saint John the Apostle, *December 27*

# U

**Undertakers,** Saint Dismis, *March 25*; Saint Joseph of Arimathea, *August 31*; Saint Nicodemus, *March 17*

**United States,** Feast of the Immaculate Conception, *December 8*

**Universal Church,** Saint Joseph, *March 19*

**Uruguay,** Saints Philip and James, *May 3*

## V

**Venereal disease,** Saint Fiacre, *August 30*

**Venezuela,** Our Lady of Coromoto

**Veterinarians,** Saint Eligius, *December 1*

**Vietnam,** Saint Joseph, *March 19*

**Vintners,** Saint Amand, *February 6*

**Vocations,** Saint Alphonsus Liguori, *August 1*

## W

**Waiters, waitresses,** Saint Martha, *July 29*

**Wales,** Saint David of Wales, *March 1*

**Weavers,** Saint Anthony Claret, *October 24*

**West Indies,** Saint Gertrude, *November 16*

**Widows,** Saint Frances of Rome, *March 9*; Saint Paula, *January 26*

**Wine trade,** Saint Amand, *February 6*; Saint Vincent of Saragossa, *January 22*

**Women in labor,** Saints Ann and Joachim, *July 26*; Saint Elmo, *June 2*

**Workers,** Saint Joseph, *March 19*

**Writers,** Saint Francis de Sales, *January 24*

## Y

**Youth,** Saint Aloysius Gonzaga, *June 21*; Saint Anthony of Padua, *June 13*; Saint John Bosco, *January 31*; Saint Joseph, *March 19*; Saint Maria Goretti, *July 6*; Saint Nicholas, *December 6*; Saint Raphael, *September 29*

# Acknowledgments

The scriptural quotations in this publication marked NRSV are from the New Revised Standard Version of the Bible, Catholic Edition. Copyright © 1993 and 1989 by the Division of Christian Education of the National Council of the Churches of Christ in the United States of America. All rights reserved.

The scriptural quotations in this publication marked GNT are from the Good News Translation® (Today's English Version, Second Edition). Copyright © 1992 by the American Bible Society. All rights reserved. Bible text from the Good News Translation (GNT) is not to be reproduced in copies or otherwise by any means except as permitted in writing by American Bible Society, 1865 Broadway, New York, NY 10023 (www.americanbible.org).

All other scriptural quotations in this book are from the New American Bible with Revised New Testament and Revised Psalms (NAB). Copyright © 1991, 1986, and 1970 by the Confraternity of Christian Doctrine, Washington, D.C. Used by the permission of the copyright owner. All rights reserved. No part of the New American Bible may be reproduced in any form without permission in writing from the copyright owner.

The excerpts marked *Catechism* and *CCC* are from the English translation of the *Catechism of the Catholic Church* for use in the United States of America, second edition. Copyright © 1994 by the United States Catholic Conference, Inc.—Libreria Editrice Vaticana. English translation of the *Catechism of the Catholic Church: Modifications from the Editio Typica* copyright © 1997 by the United States Catholic Conference, Inc.—Libreria Editrice Vaticana.

The prayers, devotions, beliefs, and practices contained herein have been verified against authoritative sources.

The excerpts from paragraph numbers 27, 1, 3, 23, 24, 25, 2, 13 and 33 from the English translation of The Order of Confirmation © 2013, International Commission on English in the Liturgy Corporation (ICEL). All rights reserved. Used with permission. Texts contained in this work derived whole or in part from liturgical texts copyrighted by ICEL have been published here with the confirmation of the Committee on Divine Worship, United States Conference of Catholic Bishops. No other texts in this work have been formally reviewed or approved by the United States Conference of Catholic Bishops.

The excerpts on pages 12, 87, and 123;18; 20; 46, 47, 50, 51, and 134; 62; 74 and

**Endnote Cited in a Quotation from the *Catechism of the Catholic Church,* Second Edition**

1. St. Irenæus, *Dem ap.* 11: Sources Chrétiennes (Paris: 1942– ) 62, 48–49.